THE HOW TO THINK LIKE LEONARDO DA VINCI WORKBOOK

Books by Michael J. Gelb

HOW TO THINK LIKE LEONARDO DA VINCI

THE HOW TO THINK LIKE LEONARDO DA VINCI WORKBOOK

SAMURAI CHESS *with Grand Master Raymond Keene*

THINKING FOR A CHANGE

LESSONS FROM THE ART OF JUGGLING *with Tony Buzan*

PRESENT YOURSELF!

BODY LEARNING

MIND MAPPING

The How to Think like Leonardo da Vinci Workbook

Your Personal Companion to
How to Think like Leonardo da Vinci

MICHAEL J. GELB

A DELL TRADE PAPERBACK

A DELL TRADE PAPERBACK

Published by
Dell Publishing
a division of
Random House, Inc.
1540 Broadway
New York, New York 10036

This book presents nutrition and exercise information which may or may not be right for you. In view of the
complex, individual, and specific nature of health and fitness problems, this book is not intended to replace
professional medical advice. Every individual is different. Before starting any diet or exercise program, get
your doctor's approval. The publisher and the author expressly disclaim any responsibility for any loss or risk
incurred as a consequence of the application of the contents of this book.

Library of Congress Cataloging in Publication Data
Gelb, Michael
The how to think like Leonardo da Vinci workbook / Michael J. Gelb.
p.   cm.
Your personal companion to : How to think like Leonardo da Vinci.
Includes bibliographical references.
ISBN 0-440-50882-7
1. Creative thinking.   2. Creative thinking—Problems, exercises, etc.
3. Leonardo, da Vinci, 1452–1519.   I. Title.
BF408.G372   1999
153.3′5—dc21   99-14091
                                                                                    CIP

Book design by Ellen Cipriano

Printed in the United States of America
Published simultaneously in Canada
June 1999
13 14 15
RRD

This workbook is dedicated to
the Da Vincian qualities of truth and beauty embodied by
my dearest friend, Nina Lesavoy.

Grazie mille to:

Ann-Marie Bolton, Jolie Barbiere, Stacy Forsythe, Michael Frederick, Ruth Kissane, John Ramo, Dr. Dale Schusterman, Audrey Elizabeth Ellzey, Dr. Roy S. Ellzey, Joshua Habermann, Murray Horwitz, Dr. Elain Jerdine, Professor Roger Paden, Ed Bassett, Charlie Bacon, Bob Ginsberg, Dave Chu, Peter Cocoziello, Jim D'Agostino, Marv Damsma, Doug Durand, Gerry Kirk, Delano Lewis, Nina Lesavoy, Joseph Rende, Dr. Raj Sisodia, the Lucent Idea Verse team, Joan and Sandy Gelb, Joan Arnold, Sir Brian Tovey, Muriel Nellis, Jane Roberts, Tom Spain, Mitch Hoffman, Jennifer Meredith, Nusa Maal, Lorraine Gill, Tony Buzan, Raymond Keene, Nicole Johns, Catherine Hillard, Debbie Ronning, Mort Herskowitz, Randi Benator, Amy Pressman, Jaya, and Julie Saunders.

Contents

WORKBOOK

NOTEBOOK

INTRODUCTION: LA DOLCE VITA

Tuscany, the land of Leonardo's birth, is the place on earth, where, as Stendhal emphasized, "the normal most regularly approaches the sublime." This quality of the sublime in everyday life is what the Italians call "La Dolce Vita," the sweet, soulful life. Why strive to think like Leonardo? Because living a sweet, soulful life in the midst of modern pressures requires the thinking, planning, and problem-solving skills of a genius.

How to Think like Leonardo da Vinci has struck a chord with aspiring Renaissance men and women around the world. The "Seven Steps to Genius Every Day" are practiced enthusiastically by people in Germany, Japan, Korea, Holland, Spain, Australia, Brazil, Poland, England, Finland, France, Italy, and throughout the United States and Canada. Why? Leonardo is, perhaps, the supreme global archetype of human potential. He represents our capacities and potential more completely than anyone who ever walked the earth. The desire to walk in the maestro's footsteps resonates with readers worldwide. Many have written and e-mailed asking for a Da Vincian Workbook/Notebook to make it easier to embody Leonardo's principles.

Bernard Berenson, the art critic who coined the term *connoisseur,* said of Leonardo that "everything he touched turned to eternal beauty." This Workbook is designed to bring more of Leonardo's touch to your life. It will make it easier to start or continue your Da Vincian journey in experience.

Walking in His Footsteps/A Personal Renaissance

Last summer, just before the book was released, I returned to Leonardo's birthplace to walk the paths that he walked and immerse myself in his spirit. I went to Anchiano where he was born and to Vinci where he spent the first years of his life. Many of the vineyards and olive groves have remained virtually unchanged through the centuries, and the fields of lavender smell the same as they did to Leonardo. In the magic of Tuscan light, the illumination of the maestro's messages became even more vivid: wake up, never stop learning, think for yourself, learn from your mistakes, refine your senses, embrace the unknown, balance your brain, "learn to preserve your health," and open yourself to the connectedness of all things.

The highlight of this pilgrimage was another visit to the Uffizi Gallery in Florence. My friend and I went at night to avoid the crowds. Our primary focus, of course, was the work of Leonardo. As we were standing again in front of the angel in the corner of Verrocchio's *Baptism of Christ,* the immaculate, luminous beauty of this creature stood out as a work of supreme genius, not only in relation to the rest of Verrocchio's *Baptism,* but also in relation to all of the masterworks in the treasure house of the Uffizi. The painting to the left, Leonardo's *Adoration of the Magi,* has to be seen in person. Reproductions just don't convey the extent of the maestro's vision. The young Leonardo once wrote "The knowledge of all things is possible!" and "I wish to work miracles!" In the *Adoration* he aims to express all his knowledge about the miracle of creation on one canvas. Viewed with his true ambition in mind, one develops a new appreciation for why this work was left unfinished.

After an hour in the Leonardo room, and another hour strolling through the galleries, we went to the "Sala de Botticelli" and did the exercise in appreciation described in the *Sensazione* chapter of *How to Think like Leonardo da Vinci*. My friend and I chose the same favorite painting (Botticelli's *Annunciation*) but we liked it for different reasons. Sharing our perspectives brought this work to life in an unforgettable way. Just before closing time we went to the rooftop cafe and shared a half bottle of champagne, some delectable chunks of parmigiano cheese, and a few fragrant strawberries. The purple-pink light of the setting sun washed over the duomo and kissed the rooftops of Florence. Although it was closing time, our waitress invited us to linger, her smile expressing her participation in the wonder of the moment. With the toasty-almond, effervescent tartness of the last swallow of champagne as accompaniment, we ran down for one last look at the Botticellis and Leonardos. Walking out into the courtyard, we were serenaded by a lone saxophonist evoking the sweet, soulful sound of nightfall. I reflected in that moment on the maestro's meditations on the way sound and aroma travel through air, and the parallels in flowing water, the curl of hair, the growth of plants, the formation of the bones and muscles, and their realtionship to movement in humans and animals; the spirit of the Leonardo's unifying vision rang true: "everything *is* connected to everything else." Suddenly, I stopped walking, overcome by a shimmering sensation from beneath my toes to beyond the top of my head. I looked up to the starlit, aubergine sky and noticed that I was standing next to a statue of Leonardo, one that I'd never seen before. A liberating inner tide of humility and gratitude washed through me. The wisdom and power of history's greatest genius seemed to be reaching out over five hundred years, urging a new renaissance. This renaissance begins one person at a time. It begins with *you*.

How to Use This Book

Think of this as two books in one: a Workbook, which you're currently reading and a Notebook, which you can find by closing this book and turning it over in your hands.

Your Da Vincian Workbook will guide you through structured practices for thinking like the maestro. Your Notebook is yours to fill, with your free-form observations, notes, poems, or any other writing or drawing. The Notebook cover is a reproduction of Leonardo's only extant self-portrait. If you turn the Notebook around and upside down, you'll be looking at the cover of your Da Vincian Workbook, and you'll see the *Mona Lisa* smiling at you. At the midpoint between your Notebook and Workbook you'll find Dr. Lillian Schwartz's brilliant computer-graphic comparison of Leonardo's self-portrait and the *Mona Lisa*. Dr. Schwartz's work demonstrates what many have intuited: that the *Mona Lisa* is a self-portrait of the maestro's soul.

Every time you work in this book, sign and date each entry. You can, of course, sign your given name, but you may also wish to occasionally sign in other ways, as Leonardo did when he signed *disciepolo della sperienza* (disciple of experience) and *uomo senza lettere* (man without letters). Make up your own *nom de plume* and have fun expressing your alter egos. If you put your heart into the exercises that follow, you'll be rewarded with a self-portrait of your own soul.

Your Da Vincian Workbook

Your Da Vincian Workbook guides you, step-by-step, through many of the exercises in *How to Think like Leonardo da Vinci* and introduces some new Da Vincian explorations as well. It also includes a mini-cookbook with sensational recipes for further enriching your experience of the third Da Vincian principle: Sensazione. Many readers have reported on their experience of practicing the exercises. As with any endeavor, the people who have put the most energy into their Da Vincian experiments report the most benefit. One critic complained that "getting through all the exercises would take a year." Actually, anyone who takes the exercises seriously will find enough to work with for at least ten years. Many of the exercises are playful and fun while others require profound reflection and inner work. You do not, of course, have to do them all, or do them in the order they are presented. The important thing is to get started, to do something. The simple choices we make every day about how we invest our time and energy determine the quality of our lives. Deepak Chopra points out that the average human has about 65,000 thoughts per day. The problem, he emphasizes, is that 95 percent of those thoughts are the same as they were yesterday! If you pursue the exercises that follow with passion, you'll change your percentage in favor of greater creativity, awareness, and quality of life. The exercises in the first six sections set the stage for you to get the most out of the final exercise in the Connessione section, where you will bring every thing together in one final exercise.

Your Da Vincian Notebook

Leonardo da Vinci carried a notebook with him at all times so that he could jot down ideas, impressions, and observations as they occurred. His notebooks (7,000 pages exist; most scholars estimate that this is about one half of the amount he left to Francesco Melzi in his will) contained jokes and fables, the observations and thoughts of scholars he admired, personal financial records, letters, reflections on domestic problems, philosophical musings and prophecies, plans for inventions, and treatises on anatomy, botany, geology, flight, water, and painting.

Written backward, Leonardo's notes are designed to be read in a mirror. Scholars debate the purpose of this "mirror writing." Some suggest it was to protect the privacy of his thoughts while others argue that it was simply a matter of convenience for a left-hander.

Notes on different subjects are frequently scribbled on the same page and many observations appear more than once, in different sections. And, of course, the pages are filled with glorious sketches, doodles, and illustrations. Although he expressed an intention to organize and publish them someday, he never got around to it. He was too busy searching for truth and beauty. But, for Da Vinci, the *process* of recording questions, observations, and ideas was of great importance.

Busy lives and job responsibilities tend to drive us toward hard conclusions and measurable results, but the exploratory, free-flowing, unfinished, nonjudgmental practice of keeping a Da Vincian Notebook encourages freedom of thought and expansion of perspective. In the manner of the maestro, don't worry about order and logical flow, just record.

You can strengthen your application of all the Da Vincian principles by working with this Notebook. Carry your Notebook with you everywhere and write in it regularly. To get the most from this book, treat it like your wallet or purse. In other words, don't leave home without it! Write in it on the bus, during a break from work, or sitting in a coffee shop. Complement your informal, spontaneous musings and observations with more "formal" sessions: Find a regular time that works for you such as first thing in the morning or last thing at night. Create a nurturing environment, surround yourself with your favorite fragrances and music, and devote a dedicated time to experiment with an exercise from the Workbook or express yourself spontaneously in your Notebook. Make this Da Vincian practice an integral part of your day and this book will become a nurturing companion, a mirror for your soul, a conduit for the whispers of your intuitive voice, and a daily celebration of your self.

Supplement your Notebook with scrapbooks or files on diverse ares of interest. Cut out and collect newspaper and magazine articles, or download information from the Internet, on any subject you fancy—science, art, music, food, health, love. . .

Like Leonardo, use your Notebook to record your questions, observations, insights, jokes, dreams, and musings (mirror writing is optional). The Notebook section is filled with inspiring quotes from Leonardo and other great geniuses of history designed to nurture your creative spirit and self-expression.

The Notebook has a simple structure designed to encourage you to apply the fifth Da Vincian principle: Arte/Scienza. The right-hand page is blank for your sketches, doodles, and mindmaps; the left-hand page is lined for your linear notes, stream-of-consciousness writings and lists. You'll find some valuable practices designed to help get the most from your Notebook throughout this Workbook.

WORKBOOK

Da Vincian explorations by

....

signature

....

date

The Seven Da Vincian Principles Are

Curiosità An insatiably curious approach to life and an unrelenting quest for continuous learning.

Dimostrazione A commitment to test knowledge through experience, persistence, and a willingness to learn from mistakes.

Sensazione The continual refinement of the senses, especially sight, as the means to enliven experience.

Sfumato (literally "going up in smoke") A willingness to embrace ambiguity, paradox, and uncertainty.

Arte/Scienza The development of the balance between science and art, logic and imagination. "Whole-brain" thinking.

Corporalita The cultivation of grace, ambidexterity, fitness, and poise.

Connessione A recognition and appreciation for the interconnectedness of all things and phenomena. Systems thinking.

In the pages that follow, you will be guided to embrace the seven Da Vincian principles in your life every day. The application of each principle begins with similar questions and statements for self-assessment introduced in *How to Think like Leonardo da Vinci*. Read and reflect on these before doing the exercises. Jot your responses to the self-assessments in the space provided. Return to them after you finish all the exercises in a section and note the ways your self-assessment has evolved.

Curiosità

An Insatiably Curious Approach to Life and an Unrelenting Quest for Continuous Learning.

"The desire to know is natural to good people."

—LEONARDO

Your Curiosità is what led you to open this Workbook . . . your desire to learn and grow is the wellspring of Da Vincian practice. And it can be developed, focused, and put to use more easily than you may have thought. First complete the self-assessment checklist below; your answers will tell you how you are already using it—and where there is room for improvement. Then cultivate your own Curiosità through the simple exercises that follow; they will focus your mind-set on growth and change, and invite an acceleration of your personal development. They also set the stage for the application of the other principles and provide fertile ground for the process of clarifying, organizing, and realizing your life goals.

Self-Assessment: Curiosità

❑ I take adequate time for contemplation and reflection.
❑ I am always learning something new.
❑ When I am faced with an important decision, I actively seek out different perspectives.
❑ I am a voracious reader.
❑ I learn from little children.
❑ I am skilled at identifying and solving problems.
❑ My friends would describe me as open-minded and curious.
❑ When I hear or read a new word or phrase I look it up and make a note of it.
❑ I know a lot about other cultures and am always learning more.
❑ I know or am learning a language other than my native one.
❑ I solicit feedback from my friends, relations, and colleagues.
❑ I love learning.

Rate yourself on Curiosità from 1–10:

Who do you know who best embodies the principle of Curiosità? Write their name or names here:

100 Questions

In the space below and on the next page, make a list of 100 questions that are important to you. Your list can include *any kind of question* as long as it's something you deem significant: anything from "How can I raise my energy level" or "How can I make more time for the people I love?" to "How can I make a difference in this world?" and "How can I deepen my faith?" Do the entire list in one sitting. Write quickly, don't worry about spelling, grammar, or repeating the same question in different words.

Review for Themes

When you have finished, read through your list and highlight the themes that emerge. Did you discover anything you did not expect? Consider the emerging themes without judging them. Are most of your questions about relationships? Business? Fun? Money? The meaning of life?

Top Ten Questions

Now choose the ten questions that seem most significant and write them in the space below. Then rank them in importance from 1–10. (Of course, you can add new questions or change the order at any time.)

Power Questions

The following questions are drawn from different people's "top-ten lists." (Perhaps you generated some similar questions in the previous exercises.) These questions are powerful catalysts to personal growth and fulfillment. Read each question and then write your answer below in stream-of-consciousness style. Then review your answers and see if they inspire an action or change you wish to make in your life. If inspiration strikes, make the change!

When am I most naturally myself? What people, places, and activities allow me to feel most fully myself, to be truly happy? What can I do to create a more supportive, enjoyable environment on a daily basis?

What is one thing I could stop doing, or start doing, or do differently, **starting today** that would most improve the quality my life? What's stopping me and how can I overcome that resistance?

What is my greatest talent? Do I use my greatest talent enough? How can I develop this talent further?

How can I get paid for doing what I love? What professions require the skills that I love? What do I need to do to pursue these professions?

Who are my most inspiring role models? Do I apply the lessons of my most inspiring role models every day? What could I do to bring more of their inspiration to my life on a daily basis?

How can I best be of service to others? What role does service play in my life today? How can I help those less fortunate than me?

What is my heart's deepest desire? Am I pursuing it every day? How can I orient my life toward my deepest passion? What's stopping me?

What are the greatest obstacles to the fulfillment of my dreams and goals? Which of those obstacles are external and which are self-imposed? How can I overcome them?

What are the blessings of my life? Do I recount them every day?

What legacy would I like to leave? Have I shared it with my family and friends so they can help me achieve it? Am I on track to leave it? What do I need to do differently to leave the legacy I choose?

What, When, Who, How, and Where? Think of a problem or question that you are concerned with in your personal or professional life. Write your question or problem statement below, and then answer the questions that follow:

What...

is the problem?

are the underlying issues?

preconceptions, prejudices, or paradigms may be influencing my perception?

will happen if I ignore it?

problems may be caused by solving this problem?

metaphors from nature can I use to illuminate it?

When...

did it start?

does it happen?

doesn't it happen?

will the consequences of it be felt?

must it be resolved?

Who...

cares about it?
is affected by it?
created it?
perpetuates it?
can help solve it?

How...

does it happen?
can I get more objective information?
can I look at it from unfamiliar perspectives?
can it be changed?
will I know that it has been solved?

Where...

does it happen?
did it begin?
haven't I looked?
else has this happened?

Why...

is it important?
did it start?
does it continue?

Ask Why, Why, Why, Why, Why . . . to get to the bottom of an
  issue.

What have you learned about your question or problem from asking
these questions? Summarize your insights below. (Use your Notebook to
do this exercise with other questions or problems. Try this exercise with
others in a group problem-solving session.)

Notebook Practice:
STREAM-OF-
CONSCIOUSNESS WRITING

A powerful complement to contemplation and theme work, stream-of-consciousness writing is a marvelous tool for plumbing the depths of your ideas, dreams, themes, questions, and musings. Choose any question or theme and, working in your Notebook, write your thoughts and associations as they occur, without editing. The secret of effective stream-of-consciousness writing is to *keep your pen moving;* don't lift it away from the paper or stop to correct your spelling and grammar, just write continuously.

Stream-of-consciousness writing yields lots of nonsense and redundancy, but can lead to profound insight and understanding. Don't worry if you seem to be writing pure gibberish; this is actually a sign that you are overriding the habitual, superficial aspects of your thought process. As you persevere, keeping your pen on the paper and moving it continuously, you'll eventually open a window through which your intuitive intelligence will shine.

Decide on a minimum time for your session, i.e., 3 minutes, 10 minutes, 20 minutes, etc.

+ Take a break after each stream-of-consciousness session.
+ Go back to your Notebook and read what you have written aloud.
+ Highlight the words or phrases that speak to you most strongly.
+ Again, look for themes, the beginnings of poems, and more provocative questions.
+ Contemplate the metaphor of the poet's motto: "Write drunk, revise sober."

Your Ideal Hobby

The quest for continuous learning is the powerhouse of the Da Vincian spirit. It is, of course, that spirit that inspires you to do the exercises in this book. You can further embrace a Da Vincian approach to life by learning a new discipline.

Most people have an "ideal" or "dream" hobby, something that they have always wanted to learn. People who pursue their dreams passionately find that life becomes richer and more fulfilling. *This exercise will help you map out a strategy for realizing your ideal hobby, now.* Make a list of your ideal hobbies. (If you are not sure what they are, make some up.)

Then choose one and ask the following questions:
What are my goals?

How will this pursuit enrich my life?

What resources will I need?

Where can I find a good teacher?

How much time will I devote to it?

What obstacles must I overcome?

If you are already doing your ideal hobby then ask: "How can I take it to the next level? How can I get paid for it?"

Feedback Exercise

Leonardo complemented his interpersonal intelligence with a lifelong commitment to developing his intrapersonal intelligence (self-knowledge). In addition to profound contemplation and reflection, Leonardo cultivated self-knowledge by seeking feedback.

You can strengthen Curiosità and deepen self-knowledge by asking your spouse, children, friends, clients, coworkers, boss, and employees for regular feedback. When you ask for feedback, be sure to listen carefully to the responses you receive, especially if they are not what you wanted or expected to hear; don't explain, justify, or argue. It's best not to comment at all, just listen and record.

Choose three people you respect and, in words that are natural to you, ask these questions, and record the responses:

- What are my weaknesses, blind spots, and areas for improvement?

- What are my strengths, my best qualities?

- What can I do to be more effective, helpful, or sensitive?

Getting pure feedback is one of the best ways to nurture Curiosità. As Leonardo wrote: **"Be desirous of hearing patiently the opinion of others, and consider and reflect carefully whether he who censures you has reason for his censure."**

Summarize what you learned from the feedback exercise here:

Dimostrazione

A Commitment to Test Knowledge
Through Experience, Persistence, and a
Willingness to Learn From Mistakes.

"The greatest deception men suffer is from their own opinions."
—LEONARDO

The real significance of the Renaissance was the transformation of fundamental assumptions, preconceptions, and beliefs. Leonardo's willingness to challenge the dominant worldview, through application of the principle of Dimostrazione, placed him in the vanguard of this revolution.

Learning to think like Leonardo requires the challenging work of questioning our own opinions, assumptions, and beliefs. Contemplate the self-assessment checklist below. These are challenging questions, but your honest reflection will help you focus on getting the most from the exercises that follow.

Self-Assessment: Dimostrazione

- ❑ Do I seek out new experiences every day?
- ❑ Am I actively pursuing different perspectives and fresh insights?
- ❑ Can I can articulate my most fundamental beliefs and the reasons I hold them?
- ❑ Have I changed a deeply held belief because of practical experience?
- ❑ Do I question "conventional wisdom" and authority?
- ❑ Do I ever practice cynicism and call it independent thinking?
- ❑ When a celebrity I admire endorses a product, am I more likely to buy it?
- ❑ Am I willing to acknowledge my mistakes?
- ❑ Would my closest friends agree that I am willing to acknowledge my mistakes? Ask them and note their responses.
- ❑ Do I learn from my mistakes, and rarely make the same one twice?
- ❑ Do I persevere in the face of obstacles?
- ❑ Am I susceptible to superstition?
- ❑ In considering new ideas, my friends and associates would say that I am: (a) gullible and "new-agey," (b) a closed-minded cynic, (c) an open-minded skeptic.

Rate yourself from 1–10 on Dimostrazione:

Think of the most independent, original thinker you know. What makes that person an original?

Examining Experience. How has experience determined your attitudes and behaviors? What are the most influential experiences of your life? Take about twenty to thirty minutes and list at least seven. Then, in one sentence, summarize what you learned from each experience.

Now spend a few minutes reflecting on how you **apply** what you have learned from these most influential experiences on an **everyday** basis. Ask yourself: "What is the single most influential experience of my life?" (For some people this is not an easy question to answer; if nothing jumps out for you, choose any experience from your list.)

How has this experience colored your attitudes and perceptions? After a few minutes of thought, summarize in a sentence or two the effects of the experience on your view of the world.

Finally, ask yourself: "Can I rethink some of the conclusions drawn at the time?" Avoid answering this last question too quickly; just hold it in your mind and heart for a while and let it "marinate."

Check Your Beliefs and Sources. How have you formed ideas, opinions, assumptions, and beliefs about areas such as: human nature, ethics, and politics. In the space provided, write down at least three beliefs you hold in the three areas you have chosen to consider, leaving room for some questions that will come later.

Topic 1

Topic 2

Topic 3

Now consider each belief and note your responses to the following questions: "How did I form this idea? How firmly do I believe it? Why do I maintain it? What would make me change my belief? Which of my beliefs inspire the strongest emotions?" Then look at each of your beliefs in the three areas you have chosen to examine and consider the role of the following sources in its formation:

Media: books, Internet, television, radio, newspapers, and magazines

People: family, teachers, physicians, religious leaders, bosses, friends, and associates

Your own experience

What criteria do you use for assessing the validity of the information you receive? Do most of your ideas come from books? Or are you primarily influenced by family? How much of what you read in the newspaper or see on television do you believe? Aim to determine, through reflection and contemplation, the dominant source of your information and the underpinnings of your beliefs and opinions. Are there beliefs that you hold for which you have no experiential verification? Is there a way you could test your convictions in experience?

In your Notebook, do a ten-minute stream-of-consciousness writing session on the following topic: "**The sources of my beliefs.**"

Notebook Practice:
BUILD YOUR OWN LEXICON

Leonardo loved learning. History's greatest genius made it a regular practice to record new vocabulary words in his notebook. In the Codex Trivulzianus and elsewhere, Leonardo noted and defined words that were of particular interest. Arranged in columns, the lists include new vocabulary, foreign terms, and neologisms.

One list included words such as:

arduous—difficult, painful

Alpine—of the region of the Alps

archimandrite—a leader of a group

After defining over 9,000 words he commented, with a delightful blend of pride and humility, "I possess so many words in my native language that I ought rather to complain of not understanding things than of lacking for words to express my thoughts properly."

This practice is a simple, powerful way to model Leonardo. Every time you discover an unfamiliar word or phrase, look it up and note it in your Notebook. Then, take every opportunity to use it in your writing and everyday conversation.

Three Points of View

When Leonardo was questing for objective knowledge—dissecting a corpse or assessing one of his paintings—he viewed his subject from at least three different perspectives. Do the same with your beliefs and opinions. Just as the maestro used a mirror to see his paintings in reverse, try making the strongest possible argument *against* your belief. Write out a statement of the belief that, in the previous exercise, generated the strongest emotion. Then summarize, as well as you possibly can, the case against your belief here:

Leonardo also sought perspective by reviewing his paintings from a distance. Try reviewing your belief "from a distance" by asking yourself: "Would my views on this change if I: lived in a different country?; came from another religious, racial, economic, or class background?; was twenty years older/younger or was a member of the opposite gender?" Choose at least one of these different perspectives and jot down your thoughts on how this different perspective might alter your belief:

Finally, seek out friends or aquaintances who you suspect might offer perspectives different from your own. Interview your friends, aiming to see the issue from another point of view. Summarize your friends' view here:

Practice Internal Anticommercial Martial Arts. As you read this book, thousands of exceptionally creative, highly focused advertising executives are marshaling budgets in the billions to influence your values, self-image, and buying habits. Preying on sexual insecurities, Walter Mitty fantasies, or just bludgeoning with pure repetition, advertisers are very good at reaching their demographic targets. From commercials for "Bud Light" to appeals for contributions to Public Broadcasting, the same basic strategies apply.

Maintaining independence of thought in the face of this onslaught requires a discipline similar to that developed through martial arts training. Go through your favorite magazine and analyze the strategy and tactics of each advertisement. Do the same analysis with the commercials from your favorite television and radio programs. Then try the following "self-defense" exercises:

Note the three advertisements that affect you most strongly; jot down your thoughts on how you are affected by each one:

Write down three messages you received from advertising when you were a child:

Make a list of the three best advertisements you have ever seen. What made them so good?

Identify three purchases you have made over the last few months, and ask yourself if you were influenced, in any way, by advertising:

In your Notebook, do a ten-minute stream-of-consciousness writing session on the topic: **"The role of advertising in the formation of my values and self-image."**

Learning from Mistakes and Adversity

Leonardo made many mistakes and experienced tremendous adversity in his quest for truth and beauty. In addition to false accusations, invasions, exile, and the wanton destruction of one of his greatest works, the maestro's most significant adversity was probably the sheer loneliness of being so far ahead of his time. Although he experienced self-doubt and questioned the value of his efforts, he never gave up. Leonardo's courage and persistence in the face of adversity are tremendously inspiring. He strengthened his will to continue his work through affirmations that he wrote in his notebook, such as:

I do not depart from my furrow.
Obstacles do not bend me.
Every obstacle is destroyed through rigor.
I shall continue.
I never tire of being useful.

Long-term studies by Dr. Martin Seligman and many others show that the critical determinant of success in business and life is resilience in the face of adversity. Awareness, deep contemplation, and a sense of humor are your best friends in attempting to live through and learn from difficult experiences.

Seligman's research also demonstrates that the ability to learn from mistakes goes hand-in-hand with resilience to adversity. Explore your attitude toward mistakes by contemplating the following questions and recording your reflections in the space provided:

At school I learned that mistakes were . . .

My parents taught me that making mistakes was . . .

The biggest mistake I ever made was . . .

The lessons I learned from that big mistake are . . .

The mistakes I repeat are . . .

The role the fear of making mistakes plays in my daily life, at work, and at home is . . .

In your Notebook try a **twenty-minute stream-of-consciousness** writing session on the topic: **"What I would do differently if I had no fear of making mistakes."**

Learn from Role Models and "Anti-Role Models"

One of the most efficient ways to learn from mistakes is to let someone else make them for you. It is wonderful to have positive role models like Leonardo who you can strive to emulate. But you can also learn a tremendous amount by studying "anti-role models." For example, I learned most of what I know about coaching and teaching from my worst coaches and teachers. I remember sitting in class while one teacher droned on endlessly; another never listened when someone asked a question; then there was the coach who was fond of humiliating his players. They taught me what *not* to do. I am also grateful to other anti-role models who, by demonstrating exactly what not to do, have helped me avoid getting into debt and having a nervous breakdown. The tricky thing about this exercise is that sometimes your greatest anti-role models also happen to be positive role models in some areas. Your task, of course, is to accurately discriminate between what you want to emulate and what you want to avoid.

List three role models and the qualities they demonstrate that you'd like to develop. What can you do today to better embody these qualities?

List three anti-role models and qualities you'd like to avoid: How can you learn from *their* mistakes?

Keep photographs and other reminders of your role models in this Notebook, your wallet or purse, hang them on the walls of your office and on the refrigerator door. Expose yourself to reminders of your highest aspirations as often as possible.

Notebook Practice: RECORD YOUR OBSERVATIONS OF PEOPLE

Leonardo nurtured his emotional intelligence by observing his fellow humans with the same passion he brought to his study of horses, birds, water, and light. As he wrote, "Oh, that it may please God to let me also expound the psychology of the habits of man in such fashion as I am describing his body!" Leonardo's deep interest in people from all walks of life is the source of the profound depth of character he illuminated in the subjects of his drawings and paintings. He counseled: "When you are out for a walk, see to it that you watch and consider other men's postures and actions as they talk, argue, laugh or scuffle; their own actions, and those of their supporters and onlookers: and make a note of these with a few strokes in your little notebook which you must always carry with you."

Leonardo's acute observations led him to a practical understanding of the art of getting along with others. He noted: "Words which fail to satisfy the ear of the listener always either fatigue or weary him: and you may often see a sign of this when such listeners are frequently yawning. Consequently when addressing men whose good opinion you desire, either cut short your speech when you see these evident signs of impatience, or else change the subject; for if you take any other course, then in place of the approbation you desire you will win dislike and ill-will."

He adds, "And if you would see in what a man takes pleasure without hearing him speak, talk to him and change the subject of your discourse several times, and when it comes about that you see him stand fixedly without either yawning or knitting his brows or making any other movement, then be sure that the subject you are speaking is the one in which he takes pleasure."

Record your observations of others; their quirks, likes and dislikes, habits and fears, body language, eye shape, and color. Use your Notebook to develop your interpersonal intelligence. Complement your written observations with sketches, drawings, and doodles.

Sensazione

The Continual Refinement of the Senses, Especially Sight, as the Means to Enliven Experience.

"The five senses are the ministers of the soul."

—LEONARDO

Think of the time in the past year when you felt most fully alive. Conjure up all the images and sensations associated with that experience. Chances are, all your senses were heightened and more focused. By refining your Sensazione, you will be able to bring the sensory aliveness of your peak experiences to your life, every day.

The exercises in this section are sensational fun. You will be tasting chocolate and wine and discovering new ways to appreciate music and art. You will learn to enrich your experience of touch and to make your own cologne, in the manner of the maestro. And, you will be introduced to synesthesia, the synergy of the senses, a secret of great artists and scientists. Underlying all the fun and pleasure is the serious purpose of refining sensory intelligence.

To get the most benefit from the delightful sensory gymnastics in this section, begin by reflecting on the self-assessment checklists—there are six in all—before proceeding to the exercises.

Self-Assessment: Vision

❏ I am sensitive to color harmonies and clashes.
❏ I know the color of all my friends' eyes.
❏ I look out into the far horizon and up to the sky at least once a day.
❏ I am good at describing a scene in detail.
❏ I like doodling and drawing.
❏ Friends would describe me as alert.
❏ I am sensitive to subtle changes in lighting.
❏ I can picture things clearly in my mind's eye.

Self-Assessment: Hearing

❏ Friends describe me as a good listener.
❏ I am sensitive to noise.

- ☐ I can tell when someone is singing off-key.
- ☐ I can sing on-key.
- ☐ I listen to jazz or classical music regularly.
- ☐ I can distinguish the melody from the bassline in a piece of music.
- ☐ I know what all the controls on my stereo system are for and can hear the difference when I adjust them.
- ☐ I enjoy silence.
- ☐ I am attuned to subtle changes in a speaker's voice tone, volume, and inflection.

Self-Assessment: Smell

- ☐ I have a favorite scent (What is it? Why do I like it? What does it remind me of?)
- ☐ Smells affect my emotions strongly, for better or worse.
- ☐ I can recognize friends by their scent.
- ☐ I know how to use aromas to influence my mood.
- ☐ I can reliably judge the quality of food or wine by its aroma.
- ☐ When I see fresh flowers, I usually take a few moments to breathe in their aroma.

Self-Assessment: Taste

- ☐ I can taste the "freshness" of fresh foods.
- ☐ I enjoy many different types of cuisine.
- ☐ I seek out unusual taste experiences.
- ☐ I can discern the flavor contributions of different herbs and spices in a complex dish.
- ☐ I am a good cook.
- ☐ I appreciate the pairing of food and wine.
- ☐ I eat consciously, aware of the taste of my food.

- ❑ I avoid junk food.
- ❑ I avoid eating on the run.
- ❑ I enjoy participating in taste tests and wine tastings.

Self-Assessment: Touch

- ❑ I am aware of the "feel" of the surfaces that surround me daily, i.e., the chairs, sofas, and car seats I sit on.
- ❑ I am sensitive to the quality of fabric that I wear.
- ❑ I like to touch and be touched.
- ❑ Friends say I give great hugs.
- ❑ I know how to listen with my hands.
- ❑ When I touch someone, I can tell if they are tense or relaxed.

Self-Assessment: Synesthesia

- ❑ I enjoy describing one sense in terms of another.
- ❑ My experience of one sense affects all my other senses.
- ❑ I intuitively understand which colors are "cold" and which are "hot."
- ❑ My response to art is visceral.
- ❑ I am aware of the role of synesthesia in the thinking of great artists and scientists.
- ❑ I can sense which of these sounds, *ooooohhlaaaa, zip-zip-zip, ni-ni-ni-ni-ni,* are reflected in the following shapes: ~`, ^ ^ ^, vvvvv.

Rank yourself 1–10 for sensory awareness on each sense.

On your self-assessments, write the name of someone you know who best represents awareness in each of the senses: Then in the space below, write a brief analysis of your sensory strengths and weaknesses:

VISION: LOOKING *AND* SEEING

You can begin to cultivate keener vision with the following practices.

The Eye-Palming Exercise. Sit at a desk in a quiet, private place. Keep your feet squarely on the floor and sit so that you are supported by the bones at the bottom of your pelvis. If you wear glasses, take them off; contact lenses are okay. Now rub your palms together vigorously for about twenty seconds. Resting your elbows lightly on the desk, cup your palms and place them gently over your closed eyes. (Do not touch the eyeball or put pressure on the sides of your nose.) Breathe deeply, in an easy, relaxed fashion, and rest with your eyes closed for about three minutes. When you are ready to finish, take your palms away from your eyes, but leave your eyes closed for another twenty seconds or so. (Do not rub your eyes!) Then gently open your eyes and look around. Write your impressions here:

Focus Near and Far. This is a very simple and valuable exercise that you can practice many times each day. Look at something close to you, such as this book or your hand; now change your focus to the farthest horizon.

Pick out a specific element of the far horizon and focus on it for a few seconds; then come back to your hand, and again out to the farthest horizon, focusing on a different element this time. In addition to enlivening your eyes and expanding your perception, this exercise can improve your driving and specifically prevent you from speeding, unknowingly, past state troopers on the freeway. Write your impressions here:

"Soft Eyes." Sitting in front of a computer screen and reading reports drives many people toward a habitually hard, narrow focus. Instead, allow a few deep exhalations and try the following exercise: Place your index fingers together at eye level about twelve inches from your face. Looking straight ahead, move your fingers slowly away from each other on the horizontal plane. Stop moving your fingers when you can no longer see them with your peripheral vision. Bring your fingers back to center and do the same exercise with the vertical plane. Exhale. Now "soften" your eyes by relaxing the muscles of your forehead, face, and jaw and allow a receptivity to the broadest possible expanse of vision. Note the way this exercise affects your mind and body (80 percent of your eyes' light receptors are designed for peripheral vision). How do you feel when you soften your eyes? Write your impressions here:

Describe a Sunrise or Sunset. Look in the newspaper to learn the exact time of the sunrise or sunset. Find a quiet place to sit where you can get a good view. Arrange to arrive at least ten minutes before the official time. Quiet your mind and body with a few deep full breaths, focusing on extended exhalations. Do the palming exercise for three minutes, then focus near and far, accessing soft eyes as you take in the horizon.

Describe the details of the experience here:

Study the Lives and Work of Your Favorite Artists. Make a list of your ten favorite painters here; explain each choice in one sentence:

Top Ten Painters of All Time

 1.
 2.
 3.
 4.
 5.
 6.
 7.
 8.
 9.
10.

Then choose one and devote a set period of time (a week, three months, a year) to immersing yourself in the study of his or her life and work. Read everything you can. Discover where you can view their works and visit them. Keep reproductions of your favorite paintings in this book; post them also in your bathroom, office, and kitchen.

Make the Most of Museums

How can you deepen your appreciation of great art and enhance your capacity for *saper vedere* (knowing how to see)? One simple key is to have a strategy for museum visits. Many very well-educated people find themselves overwhelmed by visits to art museums; without a positive strategy for viewing and enjoying an exhibition, one can often come away exhausted and unfulfilled.

Try the following: Go to a museum with a friend, each of you bringing along your Notebooks. Decide in advance which sections of the collection you wish to view. As you enter each room, split up, agreeing to exchange reactions after twenty minutes.

Suspend judgments based on all the analytical terms you may have learned in your college art history course, and avoid looking at the names of the artists or works until *after* you have taken the time to appreciate them deeply. In your notebook, identify the three paintings or sculptures in a particular room that affect you most profoundly. Explain what appeals to you about each work. Then meet with your friend and share your impressions of the most outstanding work in that room. (When I do this exercise with my friends they invariably say something like "That was the most fun I ever had in a museum!")

Notebook Practice:
DRAWING AND SKETCHING

Like Leonardo, use your Notebook for drawing, sketching, and creative doodling. Part of the beauty of working with a notebook is that it is just for you; so your drawings, sketches, and creative doodles can be pure expressions of your experience of the world rather than products for someone else to judge. Leonardo did not draw to please others. He drew because he loved it. And judging from the fact that most of his drawings were contained in his *unpublished* notebooks, he valued the process of drawing more than the finished product. As you learn to draw for yourself, you will find that you discover deeper insights and joy from the process. Of course, drawing is a skill, and, just like any other skill, it requires a desire to learn, focused attention, practice, and thoughtful instruction. Resources for developing your skill of saper *vedere* through drawing include *Drawing on the Right Side of the Brain* by Betty Edwards, *The Natural Way to Draw* by Kimon Nikolaides, *Perspective Without Pain* by Phil Metzger, *Leonardo's Ink Bottle* by Roberta Weir, and "The Beginner's Da Vinci Drawing Course" in *How to Think like Leonardo da Vinci*. (Special thanks to Nusa Maal for extensive and masterful contributions to the drawing course. And Lorraine Gill, for her inspiring ideas on shading, perspective, and perception.)

LISTENING AND HEARING

Every sound and every silence provides an opportunity to deepen auditory attunement; but city sounds can be overwhelming and cause us to dull our sensitivity. Surrounded by noises from jackhammers, televisions, airplanes, subways and automobiles, most of us "tune out" for self-protection. Try the following exercises to "tune up" your auditory sense.

Layered Listening. Enjoy a few full deep exhalations, and listen to the sounds around you now. First you'll hear the loudest, most obvious sounds: the air conditioning, the clock ticking, the traffic outside, the background noises of people and machinery. Then, as that "layer" becomes clarified, begin to notice the next layer down. Sounds of your breathing, a gentle breeze, footsteps in the hall, the shifting of your sleeve when you move your hand. Keep moving your awareness deeper into the next layer and then the next . . . do this for the next few minutes and record your observations here:

Listen for Silence. Practice listening for the spaces between sounds—in music, conversation, wherever you hear it. Find a place of complete silence. In the space below, describe how silence sounds, and how it feels to be in a place of complete quiet:

Study the Lives and Work of Your Favorite Composers and Musical Artists. Fine music is the most powerful tool for cultivating appreciation of sound and the subtleties of hearing. Leonardo referred to the art of music as "the shaping of the invisible." Apply the following tips and exercises to increase your sensitivity and enjoyment.

What's your favorite category of music? Classical? Gospel? Raga? Pick your favorite, and list your top ten composers and/or artists within that category. (You may want to put one on the CD player right now.) Write a sentence or two on why you are making each choice:

1.

2.

3.

4.

5.

6.

7.

8.

9.

10.

Choose one composer or artist from the list and immerse yourself in his or her work for a day, a week, or a month. In a few sentences below, explain how that experience enhances your appreciation of the music:

GREAT MUSIC FROM THE CLASSICAL CANON

With the help of four experts in the field, I've assembled a rough attempt at identifying what may be the ten greatest pieces from the classical canon. Listen to them and decide for yourself. We'll use them in the exercises that follow.

Bach: Mass in B Minor. If you find yourself in a depression or crisis of faith, listen to this; it will reassure you of the existence of God. Look for the version recorded by Sir Georg Solti and the Chicago Symphony.

Beethoven: Symphony No. 9. Transformation of darkness to light with a spectacular finale; Beethoven's setting of Schiller's text celebrating the brotherhood of man is awe-inspiring. Learn the words to the chorus in German and sing along.

Mozart: Requiem. Mozart's Requiem is a musical embodiment of the Resurrection. Ironically, it was finished by Mozart's student due to his untimely death.

Chopin: Nocturnes. These intimate compositions will suffuse your soul with moonlight. (Try listening to this as you drift off to sleep.)

Brahms: German Requiem. The scope of expression ranges from monumental echoes of the eternal to the extremely personal and comforting.

Mahler: Symphony No. 6. Mahler echoes the pulse of creation. This symphony celebrates the triumph of the life force!

R. Strauss: Four Last Songs. These pieces for soprano and orchestra are settings of poems by Hermann Hesse and Joseph von Eichendorff. The depiction of the soul taking flight in "Beim Schlafengehen" is one of the most extraordinary moments in all of Western music.

Debussy: Preludes. Each of these jewel-like pieces is a unique miniature characterization in an impressionistic style.

Stravinsky: "The Rite of Spring." Explosive, incendiary, and compellingly rhythmic, the audience rioted at its premier.

Verdi: *Aida* and Puccini: *La Bohème*. Everyone agreed that an operatic composition deserved a place in the top ten; but we could not agree on which one. so it's a tie. In live performance, Verdi's *Aida* will give you an unforgettable experience of the opera. For recorded listening, Puccini's *La Bohème* is hard to beat. His beautiful melodies capture the essence of romance. (All of the experts emphasized the importance of seeking out the hightest quality recordings by the finest performers and conductors.)

Listen to the Same Piece of Music Played by Different Orchestras and Conductors. For example, listen to Beethoven's Ninth Symphony played by the Berlin Philharmonic, conducted by Herbert von Karajan. Then listen to the same Beethoven played by the Boston Philharmonic Orchestra, conducted by Benjamin Zander. Describe the difference in what you hear:

Listen for Different Musicians Playing the Same Instrument. One pianist's performance of Chopin's Nocturnes will sound very different from another's, even though it's the same instrument. Pick two Nocturnes recordings by different artists. How do they interpret the pieces differently? How do they make their pianos sound different from each other? Record your observations here:

Listen for Patterns of Tension and Release

All composers, regardless of genre, employ methods that ultimately involve the creation of tension and its subsequent release; rhythmic variation, key change, rests, and harmonic movement all lead the listener along a path of motion, stillness, melodic highs and lows to the raising of musical expectations and fulfillment. Listen to one of the orchestral pieces just listed and see if you can pinpoint the key moments of momentum: building and release. Try drawing a "graph" that describes the patterns of tension and release:

Now pick one of your own favorite pieces of music and draw a similar graph:

Appreciate Music in Terms of the Elements

Leonardo and his contemporaries often viewed the world in terms of the elements: earth, fire, water, and air. Listen again to your favorite pieces in the top ten and describe them in terms of the elements:

Listen for Emotion

Some music plays with our heartstrings, and some doesn't. Which of the ten pieces in the canon affected you most profoundly? Which instruments? Voices? Choose three of the pieces and describe them in terms of the feelings they evoke:

Notebook Practice:
CONTEMPLATION

George Bernard Shaw once said, "People hate thinking. They will do almost anything to avoid it. I have made an international reputation for myself by doing it once or twice a week." In an age of sound bites, deep thinking—contemplation—is becoming a lost art. Attention spans grow shorter and the soul suffers. Contemplation, as defined by Webster, is "to look at with continued attention, to meditate on." It comes from the root *contemplari,* which means to "mark out a temple" (*con,* with; *templum,* temple) or "to gaze attentively."

Choose any question, belief, or idea inspired by your Workbook exercises or from any other source, and write it out in your Notebook, then hold it in your mind for a sustained period, at least ten minutes at a time. Then find a quiet, private place and read your question or idea over a few times.

+ Relax, breathe deeply, allowing extended exhalations.
+ Sit with your question.
+ When your mind starts to wander, bring it back by reading the question again, out loud. It is particularly valuable to do this contemplation exercise before going to sleep, and again upon waking. You will find that if you practice it sincerely, your mind will "incubate" insights overnight.
+ Record your "incubatory reflections" in your Notebook. (Do this exercise once or twice a week to build an international reputation!)

AROMATIC AWARENESS

Every day, all day, we are confronted with a smorgasbord of smells. Our five million olfactory cells can sniff out one molecule of an odor-causing substance in one part per trillion of air. And we take about 23,000 breaths per day, processing about 440 cubic feet of scent-laden air.

But most people have a very limited vocabulary for describing aromatic experience: "It stinks" or "That smells good" are the most common references. Aim to increase your discrimination and appreciation for smell by expanding your olfactory vocabulary. Perfumers categorize smells as floral (roses), minty (peppermint), musky (musk), ethereal (pears), resinous (camphor), foul (rotten eggs), and acrid (vinegar). Use these terms and make up your own descriptors as you explore the following exercises.

What Do You Smell Right Now? In the manner of your most beloved canine aquaintance, explore your immediate environment with your nose. Breathe in the smell of the surrounding air, your shirt, a pencil or pen, or the pages of this Workbook. Describe what you smell, right now, as vividly as you can. Describe your experience here:

Make "Smells" a Theme for a Day. Record what you smell and how it affects you through the course of a day. Most people find that smell has a powerful effect on their emotions and memory. Seek out unusual or intense aromas. Spend half an hour at your favorite florists. Make a scent-centered visit to your nearest zoo. Inhale the aroma of ten different perfumes and describe your reactions. How does smell affect your moods? Your memory? List three specific examples of aromas affecting your emotion or recall:

Olfactory Cornucopia. This exercise is easier and more fun to do with friends. Assemble a range of items with distinctive aromas; for example,: a slice of lemon, a piece of sod, a few leaves of basil, your pillowcase, some Tiger Balm or Vicks VapoRub, freshly ground coffee, a jar of capers, a piece of charcoal. Put on a blindfold and ask a friend to hold each item, in turn, close to your nose for thirty seconds. Describe each smell and your reaction to it:

Make Your Own Perfume. Go to a fragrance shop and sample essential oils: lavender, patchouli, clove, rose, eucalyptus, and so on. Invest in as many as you can. How does each fragrance affect you? How does it affect your friends? Experiment with different combinations and make your own favorite scent.

GOOD TASTE

For most of us, the opportunity to taste presents itself at least three times a day. But in the rush of our lives, it is often difficult to pay attention. It is all too easy to "grab a bite on the run," and to consume an entire meal without really tasting anything. Instead, pause for a few moments before every meal. Reflect on the origins of the meal you are about to enjoy. Aim to be 100 percent present as you taste the first bite of your food.

Comparative Tasting

Just as comparing one great performance to another is a marvelous way to develop your hearing, the same holds true for taste and smell. Buy three different kinds of chocolate (i.e., dark, milk, semisweet). Begin by looking carefully at each one and describing any differences you observe in color or clarity. Then smell each one for thirty seconds. Describe the aromas. Next taste each one in turn; hold a piece in your mouth and let it melt on your tongue. Take a sip of springwater between tastes to clear your palate. Describe the differences in aroma and taste:

1.

2.

3.

Try the same comparison process with three different kinds of olive oil, mushrooms, beer, apples, bottled water, smoked salmon, caviar, grapes, or vanilla ice cream. Record your impressions here:

1.

2.

3.

1.

2.

3.

Wine Tasting

Fine wine is art you can drink. Learning to appreciate and enjoy wine is the most powerful and delightful way to refine your sense of smell and taste. (If you choose not to drink alcohol, you can try the following exercises with the nonalcoholic wines produced by Ariel, St. Regis, and others.)

To hold a succesful wine tasting you need a harmonious, well-lit environment so you can appreciate the color of the wine (purists insist on white tablecloths so as not to distract from the color of the wine); a basket of crusty bread and some springwater to clear your palate between tastes of different wines; good wineglasses engineered to optimize aroma and taste (the best are made by Reidel Crystal). And, of course, a corkscrew and some fine wine.

Organize your tasting around a theme. Try, for example, comparing a top-level California chardonnay, pinot noir, or cabernet sauvignon with a similarly priced white burgundy, red burgundy, or Bordeaux from France. Or taste three different vintages of Chianti, from Leonardo da Vinci's homeland, the Tuscan region of Italy. (Try the Antinori Chianti Classico Tenuta Riserva. The Antinori family were established Tuscan winemakers when Leonardo was born in 1452. The 1990, 1993, and 1995 are the best currently available vintages.)

Although tasting is the central pleasure of wine, all the senses play a role in its full enjoyment: the feel of the bottle in your hand, the perfect sound of the cork's exit, the texture of the cork in your fingers, the gurgle of the wine as it fills your glass. Hold your glass up to the light and gaze at the color of your wine; then swirl the wine around to release its volatile aromatics. Plunge your nose into the glass and savor its smell. Take your time enjoying the aroma and describing its elements. Then drink, swishing the wine around your palate, appreciating the tastes, textures, and feel in your mouth. Swallow, and notice the flavors and sensations that linger. This last element, called the "finish," is the supreme mark of a great wine. The finest wines send surges of pleasure through your mouth for a full minute after swallowing.

Try a comparative tasting. Start with two wines and record your observations below. Describe each stage of the tasting process precisely and poetically:

	wine #1	wine #2
Color		
Aroma		
Texture in the mouth		
Taste		
Finish		
Gestalt (the whole experience)		

As you gain experience in wine tasting, you'll find that your appreciation for other tastes and smells is heightened. *Salud! Cent'anni!*

TOUCHING AND FEELING

Your brain receives information from more than 500,000 touch detectors and 200,000 temperature sensors. Yet Leonardo lamented that most people "touch without feeling." The secret of sensitive "feeling" touch is an attitude of receptivity, learning to "listen" deeply with your hands and whole body.

Touch Like an Angel. Imagine the quality of touch that Leonardo used in applying the gossamer layers of paint in creating his angels and virgins. Now, with the exquisite delicacy of the maestro as your inspiration, touch the objects around you. Touch the world around you as though you were experiencing each sensation for the first time. Record your observations here (include your description of the feeling of your pen in your hand as you write):

Enjoyable Touch

Notice the quality of different people's touch: the firmness of a handshake, the warmth of a hug, the softness of a kiss. Aside from lovemaking, think of the most enjoyable touch you have ever felt. What made it so good? Jot down your thoughts here:

How can you bring more of the quality of touch that you love the most to others? Give a friend a foot massage, and schedule a massage for yourself, to get the most from this theme. Describe your experiences below:

Blindfold Touch. Invite a friend to share this exercise. Assemble as many of the following objects as you can find: a leather jacket, a cashmere scarf, a glass, a potato, a rose, a handful of coins, a scouring pad, a sponge, a dab of moisturizing cream, your friend's hand. and anything else you would like to explore. Put on a blindfold and explore them all with with receptive, listening hands. Describe the textures, weight, temperature, and other sensations here:

Touch Nature. Go outside and explore the textures of nature: the needles of a pine tree, rocks and stones, flowing water, the wind, the earth at your feet. Record your observations here:

Make "Touch" a Theme for the Day

Record your observations in your Notebook.

SYNESTHESIA

Synesthesia, the merging of the senses, is a characteristic of great artistic and scientific geniuses.

You can heighten all your powers of Sensazione by cultivating synesthetic awareness. A simple way to begin is to practice describing one sense in terms of the others. Try the following exercises for developing synesthesia.

Drawing Music. Listen to your favorite piece of music. As you listen, experiment with expressing your impressions by drawing shapes and colors here:

Shaping the Invisible. If you were to sculpt a particular piece of music, what materials would you use? What shapes would you make? Which colors? How would the music smell? If you could bite into the music, what would it taste like? Try this imaginary multisensorial sculpting exercise with at least two of your favorite pieces of music.

Sounds of Color. Look at a reproduction of your favorite painting. Vocalize the sounds inspired by the colors, shapes, and textures on the canvas.

Transpositions. Review your list of great artists and composers. Imagine transposing them based on their work, not their personalities. In other words, if Picasso were a composer who would he be? If Aaron Copland were a painter, who would he be? For example, perhaps, if Picasso were a musician he would be Stravinsky; and if Copland were a painter he might be Andrew Wyeth. This is a delightful exercise to do with friends. After everyone has offered a few transpositions, ask each person to explain their choices.

Synesthetic Problem-Solving. Think back to one of the questions you worked with in Curiosità. Give it a color, shape, and texture. Imagine what it smells and tastes like. How does it feel? What are the textures, tastes, shapes, colors, and sounds of some possible solutions?

Synesthetic Cookbook

Many readers enjoyed the recipe for "synesthetic minestrone" introduced in *How to Think like Leonardo da Vinci* and asked for more. The following recipes, all tested and refined in my kitchen, are based on the fundamental philosophy of Italian cooking as handed down from Grandma Rosa, Aunt Virginia, and my mom. This philosophy can be interpreted as follows. Take the best ingredients and don't mess them up! In other words, when you prepare a fabulous meal, it should be abundantly clear that the credit goes to God, nature, your ancestors, or the Tao.

Dining is a simple and sacred act of communion with nature, self, and family or friends. Two or three times a day you have the opportunity to pause, give thanks, and immerse yourself in an experience of sensazione. The tastes, smells, textures, sounds, and sights of a good meal are one of life's most reliable pleasures for those of us fortunate enough to live amid unprecedented abundance. The cuisines of the world offer a most delectable door to developing synesthetic aliveness and global awareness. One Da Vincian enthusiast, inspired by the desire to cultivate Sensazione, Curiosità, and Connessione for his children, wrote that he and his wife created international theme weeks for their family meals: choosing a different country every week, they served the food, tasted the wine, listened to the music, and learned some history and a few words of the language of the culture they were "dining in." They began, as you might like to, with an Italian week, and took the whole family to "Little Italy" for their food-shopping and cultural enrichment.

As you prepare these recipes, embrace a Sensazione approach to cooking and dining; use all your senses to enhance your enjoyment of every meal while improving your talents in the kitchen. This approach begins with careful shopping; there is no substitute for finding good ingredients. "Knowing how to see" is the beginning of effective food-shopping; train yourself to recognize the visual signs, and then the smells and textures, of freshness and goodness in all things. (If you don't have a Grandma Rosa to teach you, then go to the best food markets and ask for help or go shopping with someone you know who is a great cook and ask him or her how to recognize the best ingredients.)

If you are just starting to learn to cook, you may want to rely on good recipes, but the real fun of the Sensazione approach is using your creative-sensory imagination to become an "Inventore" in the kitchen. The secret of this approach is cultivating your ability to imagine what a dish will look, smell, feel, and taste like, and comparing imagined reults with what you know of the tastes and preferences of the people for whom you are cooking. In addition to visualizing the sensory experience of each dish, you also imagine the way one dish prepares the palate and digestive system of your guest for the next, and ultimately the overall experience of the harmony of food, wines, and ambiance.

How to Cook like Leonardo da Vinci

You can use the seven Da Vincian principles to guide the process of creating a great meal as follows:

Curiosità—As you prepare to create your menu, ask questions like "What are the likes and dislikes of my guests? What's in season?" As you walk through the food market ask: "What looks the freshest and most delicious? How can I combine the most inviting ingredients into a wonderful, new symphony of textures, aromas, colors, and flavors?"

Dimostrazione—What does my experience and intuition guide me to prepare? What mistakes should I avoid?

Sensazione—How can I orchestrate the aromas, textures, colors, and flavors for maximum delight? How can I create the most appetizing environment?

Sfumato—Can I embrace the tension of not knowing exactly how things will turn out?

Arte/Scienza—Do I know where to follow science (i.e., the recipe) and where I can let my imagination run wild (arte)?

Corporalita—Am I creating and serving a healthy, balanced meal? How will my guests and I feel after we eat?

Connessione—Have I visualized the way each thing I am preparing will connect with everything else? Do I take time to give thanks, appreciate the source of this blessing, be in the moment, and savor every aroma and taste of this experience?

Appetizers/Antipasti

Three olive oils and bread: Start your meal with an olive oil tasting. Pour each oil on a small white plate (best for appreciating the different shades of color). Enjoy the differences in color, aroma, viscosity, taste, and aftertaste.

Three kinds of olives: Try a "tasting" of olives, with a bite of good Italian bread between each type. Compare, for example, tiny Niçoise, mid-sized oil-cured Thasos, and giant green Cerignola olives. Olives are delicious and very appetizing, best washed down with champagne or a crisp sauvignon blanc.

Chunks of parmigiano cheese and crusty bread: Cut or break the cheese into bite-size chunks and eat it with your fingers. Perfect accompaniment for champagne or fine wine.

Buffalo mozzarella, tomatoes, and basil: This is a classic Italian appetizer that is beautiful, luscious, and easy to prepare. Slice the cheese and tomatoes and layer them with the basil along a simple white platter. Grate some black pepper and then drizzle a little olive oil on top (for a marvelously decadent variation, use white truffle oil . . . it's expensive but a little goes a long way).

Scallops, oyster mushrooms, and asparagus: Use 2 or 3 large diver scallops per person, 3 or 4 oyster mushrooms (sliced), and 3 or 4 pieces of asparagus. Steam the asparagus until they are al dente and squeeze on a bit of lemon juice. Sauté the mushrooms slowly in butter and garlic. Put the asparagus and mushrooms on each plate. Then sauté the scallops on low to medium heat in butter and a little bit of the chardonnay that you are planning to drink with this course. Stop cooking the scallops before the center turns milky white (they are overcooked at this point; the center should have a pinkish hue. Remember that things keep "cooking" for a minute or two even after you take them off the stove or out of the oven). Serve the scallops with a little sprinkle of paprika and savor the textures and taste of this dish with the best chardonnay you can buy . . . the combination is heaven!

Warm oyster and arugula salad: Buy some fresh, shucked oysters. Marinate them in some lemon juice and a splash of good white wine or champagne. Sauté a few cloves of garlic in a little butter/olive oil mix. Pour in a few gurgles of good white wine or champagne. Let the wine and oil/butter mix together, then gently guide the oysters into the pan. The moment the oysters become warm in the center, ladle them on top of individual bowls of arugula, dust with fresh black pepper, and serve immediately.

I primi/pasta and risotto In Italian cooking, the "I primi" or first course is usually a pasta, risotto, or soup. The antipasto whets the appetite and this course takes the edge off your hunger. Of course, all of these dishes can be served as main courses as well. Here are a few favorites:

❧ Linguini with Fresh Clams and Black Truffles

Preparation time: 20 minutes
Serves 2–4

INGREDIENTS:

½ box linguine (DeCecco makes the best readily available dried pasta)
½ to ¾ pound fresh clams (this dish is also great with rock shrimp if you can't find the fresh clams)
A couple of small black truffles (Urbani sells them two to a jar for about eight dollars)
A few cloves garlic
A little good white wine
A few tablespoons olive oil (ideally suffused with truffle!)
Juice of half a lemon
A hint of hot paprika

Sauté the clams over a very low flame with some olive oil and garlic, pour in the white wine and lemon juice. Slice in the truffles and pour in a bit more oil. Simmer until you are overcome with desire. Pour it on the freshly cooked pasta, add a touch of hot paprika, and garnish with Italian parsley.

Formaggio alert: Many authorities on Italian cuisine discourage putting grated cheese on seafood dishes. In the spirit of Dimostrazione, experiment for yourself and find out if you agree.

A note on cooking with wine: Never use "cooking wine"; if the wine isn't good enough to drink, do not put it in your food. Although the subtleties of the very finest wines are, of course, compromised in cooking, they nevertheless impart some of their mystery and delight to your recipe.

❧ Capellini with Tuscan-pepper Sauce

Preparation time: about 15 minutes
Serves 2–4

INGREDIENTS:

1/2 box capellini
About 15 Tuscan peppers (Kronos is the best brand)
5-6 cloves garlic
A few tablespoons olive oil
1/4 pound butter
Freshly ground black pepper
Freshly grated pecorino chesse

Crush the garlic and chop the Tuscan peppers into three or four pieces. Sauté garlic and peppers in olive oil on a low flame until the garlic just starts to turn brown. In a separate pan, melt the butter. Cook and drain your capellini (it doesn't take long to overcook it!). Pour the melted butter on the pasta, toss in a handful of pecorino cheese, and mix it around. Grind some fresh black pepper on top and then pour on the hot pepper/garlic mix. Stir and let it sit for a couple of minutes.

Writing about this dish makes me salivate! The heat, and cool crunch, of the crispy Tuscan peppers complemented by the smack of black pepper and garlic on the nose and the sumptuousness of the oil-butter-pasta-pecorino base makes this bowl of pasta a peak experience.

Pairing Food and Wine. Everyone says white with fish, red with meat, except that reds sometimes go beautifully with fish and whites are often perfect with veal. Practice Dimostrazione and discover your own preferences. If your wine is good enough, then you don't have to worry too much about what you eat with it . . . great wine goes with everything! Of course, there are some wonderful pairings that always seem to delight most palates. Here are three of the best: **Seafood, especially oysters, and sauvignon blanc:** Look for Sancerre from the Loire Valley, wines like Matanzas Creek, Caymus, and Mondavi from California, and, the ultracrisp delightful renditions of this grape from New Zealand. **Foie gras and sauterne muscat de beaumes devenise:** For a taste of heaven, slather a small amount of duck or goose liver on some lightly toasted walnut-fig bread, serve it with a small glass of sauterne from Bordeaux (best in great years like 1986, 1988, or 1990)—such as Château Climens, Lafaurie-Peyrarguey, or Rieussec—or, less expensively, with a muscat from the Rhône, like the one made by Paul Jaboulet. This combination is also heavenly with a rare wine from Maculan in Italy called Acininobili. **Vintage Port and Stilton, Roquefort, or Gorgonzola:** Have this after dinner or on a winter afternoon in front of a fireplace. Fonseca, Taylor, and Grahams are the kings of Oporto. Look for 1963, 1977, 1983, or 1985 for drinking now; buy 1992 and 1994 and save them for ten years.

❧ Lemon-Pepper Fettuccine with Artichoke Heart Pesto

Preparation time: 45 minutes
Serves 4–8

INGREDIENTS:

One box lemon-pepper fettuccine
16 artichoke hearts (sliced into quarters)
⅓ cup pine nuts
Juice of half a lemon
A few tablespoons olive oil
8 cloves of garlic
A small jalapeño pepper (sliced into 6–8 pieces)
A handful of grated pecorino

Crush all the solid ingredients with a mortar and pestle (more sensual, aromatic, and fun than a food processor). Mix in the liquid and stir it all around. Let it sit for half an hour. Cook and drain your pasta (if you can't find lemon-pepper fettuccine, plain or red-pepper fettuccine will also do nicely). Pour on some melted butter or olive oil. Mix your pesto in thoroughly. Let it sit for a couple of minutes and then enjoy!

❧ Greek Fusilli

Preparation time: 20 minutes
Serves 4–8

INGREDIENTS:

½ box regular fusilli
½ box spinach fusilli
A big block of crumbled feta cheese

12 artichoke hearts (sliced into quarters)
About 20 pitted calamata olives
About ⅓ jar minced sun-dried tomatoes
Hot pepper flakes

Warm up all the ingredients by simmering them in olive oil and garlic. Cook the pasta and mix in all the ingredients.

❧ Risotto with Wild Mushrooms

Preparation time: about 30 minutes
Serves 4

INGREDIENTS:

1½ cups Italian Arborio rice
1 or more shallots
Some good white wine or champagne
1 quart chicken broth
Wild mushrooms: shiitake, cremini, portobello, morels,
  chanterelles, etc.
Extra splurge: white truffle oil
A handful of freshly grated parmigiano cheese

Sauté the mushrooms in butter and garlic and put them aside. Sauté the shallots in olive oil until they are translucent. Sprinkle in the rice and stir it around until it is completely coated with the olive oil. Add a little wine and stir gently over a low-medium flame. When the wine is absorbed, add the chicken broth in three or four "installments," waiting until it is absorbed each time before adding more. (The secret of great risotto is finding the best rice and then orchestrating the rate of absorption by controlling the relationship between heat, stirring, and amount and timing of liquid added.) When the rice is just about ready (not crunchy but not mushy), add the mushrooms and cheese and stir them in gently. Serve in a small bowl with a drizzle of white truffle oil on top.

I SECONDI/ MAIN COURSES

❧ Tonno Festivale

Preparation time: 20-30 minutes
Serves 4

INGREDIENTS:

4 of the best tuna steaks you can find
8 slices fresh ginger
8 cloves garlic (crushed)
2 shallots (chopped)
A splash of balsamic vinegar
A splash of dark soy sauce
Black pepper
Sliced red and green jalapeño peppers
¼ cup champagne or good white wine

Marinate the tuna in the ginger, garlic, shallots, balsamic vinegar, soy sauce, black and jalapeño peppers, and wine combination for a few hours. Sauté it until it's medium rare (don't overcook!!). Serve with a side dish of capellini with basil pesto.

A Little Cooking Music, Please

Experiment with finding your favorite musical accompaniment for preparing each dish. When cooking an Italian feast, or even a simple bowl of pasta, you might enjoy listening to Andrea Bocelli's "Romanza," "Viaggio Italiano," and "Aria"; other classics include "The Three Tenors" and Luciano Pavarotti's version of Puccini's greatest hits; also, the soundtracks from *Big Night*, *The Godfather*, and just about anything from Frank Sinatra, Bobby Darin, or Tony Bennett.

❧ Duck Breast with Sorrel and Raspberries

Preparation time: 20 minutes
Serves 2

INGREDIENTS:

2 duck breasts (if you can't shoot your own duck, D'Artagnan is
  a wonderful brand)
4–6 sorrel leaves
$^1/_4$ cup fresh raspberries
Marinate for an hour or two in a $^1/_4$ cup of good red zinfandel,
  a splash of cherry brandy or cassis, crushed black pepper.

Shred the sorrel leaves and sauté them in butter. Sear the duck breasts
in the sorrel butter and then finish them on the grill or broiler. Pour the remaining sorrel butter over the duck and then sprinkle a handful of fresh
raspberries on top.

(If you like duck and don't have time to prepare the dish above, buy
d'Artagnan's confit of duck. It consists of a marinated and precooked leg
and thigh that fall off the bone. Open the package, heat it under your
broiler, and serve it with a side dish of spinach or Swiss chard in garlic.
Your guests will think that you slaved in the kitchen for hours.)

Desserts

Formaggio. Cheese with a bit of fresh (apples, pears, grapes) and/or
dried (figs, apricots, cherries) fruit and a few unsalted walnuts, pecans,
and/or almonds is a perfect accompaniment for your best red wine or port
and a magnificent way to end your meal. Experiment with Gorgonzola,
Stilton, Roquefort, and Chèvre (goat cheese). Ask for guidance at the best
cheese store you can find. Be sure to serve cheese at room temperature.

Fresh Figs Soaked in Tawny Port with a Touch of Fresh Cream and Plain Biscotti. Find some fresh, ripe purple figs at your local gourmet store or fruit specialist. Slice them in half and soak them for at least a few hours in a good tawny port (Australian tawnys are great and inexpensive, about $10 a bottle). Serve with a touch of fresh cream and a plain biscotti to dip in the fig/port juice.

Hammered Bittersweet Chocolate and Espresso. This is a simple and dramatically delicious desert. Espresso and chocolate represent magnificently concentrated expressions of the earth's bounty. Buy a block of dark Mexican, Belgian, or Valhrona chocolate, wrap it in wax paper and then in a kitchen towel. Pound it with a hammer and serve the chocolate shards with the best espresso.

Become One with the Garlic!

Before you chop, cut, mince, slice, grind, crush, dice, steam, sear, boil, sauté, bake, poach, or grill your ingredients, hold each one in your hands and savor its weight, texture, shape, and color. Breathe in the aromas of each ingredient and sing or hum the notes of its essence. Observe and enjoy each phase of preparation and the synthesis of juices, herbs, and spices. Inhale the colors of each ingredient, express the aromas in gesture; articulate what you see in vivid, spontaneous poetry. As you cross-reference your senses and express your experience, everything becomes more vivid, memorable, and enjoyable.

Notebook Practice:
CULTIVATE AN EYE FOR NOSES

Leonardo suggested the following exercise in "knowing how to see":". . . first learn by heart the various kinds of heads, eyes, noses, mouths, chins, throats, and also necks and shoulders. Take as an instance noses: they are of ten types: straight, bulbous, hollow, prominent either above or below the center, aquiline, regular, simian, round and pointed. These divisions hold good as regards profile. Seen from in front, noses are of twelve types: thick in the middle, thin in the middle, with the tip broad, and narrow at the base, and narrow at the tip, and broad at the base, with nostrils broad or narrow, or high or low, and with the openings either visible or hidden by the tip. And similarly you will find variety in the other features; of which things you ought to make studies from nature and fix them in your memory."

Following the maestro, take "Faces" as a theme for the day. Then on a subsequent day take "Noses" as a theme. Sketch the different types in profile and from the front. Then do the same with "Eyes" "Mouths," etc.

Leonardo wrote, "The lover is drawn by the thing loved, as the sense is by that which it perceives." Drawing, in the manner of the maestro, is making love with the world through your eyes.

Sfumato

(Literally "going up in smoke")
A willingness to Embrace Ambiguity,
Paradox, and Uncertainty.

"That painter who has no doubts will achieve little."
—LEONARDO

While this Workbook was being written, the American President was impeached, Iraq and Yugoslavia were bombed, British Petroleum bought Amoco, and the NBA season was almost canceled. Meantime, a single currency was introduced in Europe, a Korean researcher announced the cloning of human cells, as global weather shifts and uncertainties about Y2K were receiving increasing media attention. In the past, a high tolerance for uncertainty was a quality to be found only in great geniuses like Leonardo. Now, as change accelerates, ambiguity multiplies, and illusions of certainty become more difficult to maintain, the ability to thrive with ambiguity must become part of our lives every day. Poise in the face of paradox is a key, not only to effectiveness, but to sanity, in a rapidly changing world.

Rate yourself on a scale of 1–10 on tolerance for ambiguity, 1 representing complete maniacal need for certainty at all times, 10 representing an enlightened Taoist priest or Leonardo. What behaviors could you change to move up one point on the scale? You'll learn more from the self-assessment that follows.

Self-Assesment: Sfumato

❑ I am comfortable with ambiguity.
❑ I am attuned to the rhythms of my intuition.
❑ I thrive with change.
❑ I see the humor in life every day.
❑ I have a tendency to "jump to conclusions."
❑ I enjoy riddles, puzzles, and puns.
❑ I usually know when I am feeling anxious.
❑ I spend sufficient time on my own.
❑ I trust my gut.
❑ I can comfortably hold contradictory ideas in my mind.
❑ I delight in paradox and am sensitive to irony.
❑ I appreciate the importance of conflict in inspiring creativity.

Sensing Ambiguity

In the space below, briefly describe three situations from your life, past or present, where ambiguity reigns:

Ambiguity Situation #1

Ambiguity Situation #2

Ambiguity Situation #3

Now that these experiences are on your mind, describe the feeling of ambiguity:

How do you physically experience ambiguity? Where in your body do you feel it? Draw your physical experience of ambiguity:

If ambiguity had a shape, what would it be? A color? A sound? A taste? A smell?

How do you respond to feelings of ambiguity?

How are ambiguity and anxiety related?

Observing Anxiety

For many people ambiguity equals anxiety; but most people, unless they have worked intensively with a good psychotherapist, do not know when they are anxious. They react to anxiety with some form of automatic avoidance behavior such as excessive talking, pouring a drink, reaching for a cigarette, or obsessive fantasy. To thrive with uncertainty and ambiguity we must learn, first of all, to know when we are anxious. As we become conscious of our anxiety, we can learn to accept it, experience it, and free ourselves from limiting compulsions of thought and action.

Describe the feeling of anxiety here:

Are there different types of anxiety? Describe them:

How do you physically experience anxiety? Where in your body do you feel it? Draw your physical experience of anxiety:

If anxiety had a shape, what would it be? A color? A sound? A taste? A smell?

How do you respond to feelings of anxiety?

Make "anxiety" a theme for a day. Record your observations in your Notebook.

Monitoring Intolerance for Ambiguity

Count the number of times in a day that you use an absolute, such as "totally," "always," "certainly," "must," "never," and "absolutely." Write a few examples below:

Balancing Tolerance for Ambiguity with Decisiveness

Some people are too good at tolerating ambiguity, and will do almost anything to avoid making a decision; others can't bear uncertainty and act prematurely. Contemplate your own tendencies. Are you more likely to act too soon or too late? How can you cultivate the ability to act at just the right time?

List three situations in which you acted prematurely and three in which you waited too long. What would you have done differently in each situation? Is there any way you could have known that you were either premature or late in your decision/action?

Curiosità Equals Uncertainty. Sfumato flows from Curiosità. As you become more curious, and intensify your desire to learn and create, you will experience more uncertainty. The willingness to embrace the unknown is one of the most distinguishing qualities of genius and Leonardo had more of it than anyone. Awaken your own everyday genius by returning to your list of your ten most important life questions from the Curiosità section. Which ones cause you the greatest sense of uncertainty or ambivalence? Are there paradoxes at the heart of any of these questions?

Try some abstract art: Sketch the feeling of uncertainty generated by the most anxiety-producing question from your Curiosità list. Use your abstract art as the central image of an exploratory mind map on your question. Write your anxiety-producing question at the top of the next page and do your abstract drawing underneath; fill the page with free-form expression, then condense it into a central image for your mind map on the following page.

Bias to Action

Creative people have a bias toward action and are more likely to ask for forgiveness than permission. They learn by doing things and live with the uncertainty of the outcomes of their decisions. The bias toward action means that creative people make more mistakes, but they apply the principle of Dimostrazione to learn the most from every mistake, thereby cultivating a fertile ground for experience-based intuition.

Cultivating Confusion Endurance

The Sfumato principle touches the essence of being, and asks us to sharpen our senses in the face of paradox and embrace creative tension. Contemplate the following paradoxes.

Joy and Sorrow. Think of the most joyful moments of your life, and the moments most filled with sadness. What is the relationship between these states? Do you ever feel joy and sorrow simultaneously? Leonardo once wrote, "The highest happiness becomes the cause of unhappiness. . . ." Do you agree? Is the opposite true? Note your reflections here:

Intimacy and Independence. In your closest relationships, what is the connection between intimacy and independence? Can you have one without the other? Does this connection ever inspire anxiety? What changes can you make in your attitudes or actions to discover a more harmonious balance between these poles? Note your reflections here:

Strength and Weakness. List at least three of your strengths as a person. List three or more of your weaknesses. How are the qualities in your lists related?

Good and Evil. Is it possible to be good without acknowledging and understanding one's own impulses toward evil, what Jung called the "Shadow"? What happens when people are unconscious of or deny the shadow? How can you recognize and accept your own prejudice, hate, anger, jealousy, envy, greed, pride, and sloth without acting it out? Note your reflections here:

Change and Constancy. Note three of the most significant changes you have observed in your lifetime. Note three things that remain constant. Is the idea that "the more things change, the more they remain the same" true or false in your experience?

Changes 1

2

3

Constant 1

2

3

Humility and Pride. Think of the proudest moments of your life. Remember the times you felt most humble. How are the feelings of genuine humility and true pride different? Are there any unexpected similarities between humility and pride? Are these qualities opposites? Note your reflections here:

Goals and Process. Think of an important goal that you have accomplished, and describe the process you followed in achieving that goal. How do goal and process relate? Have you ever achieved a success without experiencing fulfillment? Does the end justify the means? How would you answer the following? To live a succesful and fulfilling life one must: (1) be one-hundred percent committed to achieving clearly defined goals; or (2) recognize that the process of living every day, the daily quality of life, is of greatest importance; or (3) both 1 and 2. Note your reflections here:

Meditate on *Mona*. Leonardo's *Mona Lisa* is so familiar that it is rarely seen. Close the book and sit with *Mona* for a while. Wait for your analytical mind to calm down and breathe in her essence. When you're ready, reopen the book and note your responses here:

Embody *Mona*'s Smile. Experiment with embodying her facial expression, especially the famous smile. Note how you feel.

Now go back to the most anxiety-producing questions from your Curiosità list. Only this time, when you think about each question, embody *Mona*'s smile. Record your observations here: Does your thinking change when you look from *Mona*'s perspective?

Incubation and Intuition

Leonardo wrote that "the greatest geniuses sometimes accomplish more when they work less." The spaces between your conscious efforts provide a key to creative living and problem solving. These spaces allow perceptions, ideas, and feelings to incubate.

Almost everyone has experienced "sleeping on a problem" and awakening with a solution. Incubation is most effective when you alternate, like Leonardo did, between periods of intense, focused work and rest; without periods of intense, focused work, there is nothing to be incubated.

Discovering and learning to trust your incubatory rhythms is a simple secret of accessing your intuition and creativity. Think of your life today. Where are you when you get your best ideas? Write down the times and places here:

Although Da Vinci loved exchanging ideas with others, he knew that his most creative insights came when he was alone. He wrote: "The painter must be solitary. . . For **if you are alone you are completely yourself,** but if you are accompanied by a single companion you are half yourself." Nurture Sfumato by taking time for solitude. Take a little time, at least once or twice a week, to go for a walk or just sit quietly by yourself. Keep this book with you and record your insights, Aha!s, and best ideas as they emerge in the Notebook section.

Schedule Breaks

You can increase your enjoyment and effectiveness, when working or studying, by taking breaks every hour or so. Modern psychological research shows that when you study or work for an hour, and then take a complete break for ten minutes, your recall for the material you have been working on is higher at the end of the ten-minute break than it was at the end of the hour. In his *Treatise on Painting,* Da Vinci counseled ". . . it is well that you should often leave off work and take a little relaxation because when you come back to it you are a better judge . . ." Follow Leonardo's advice and build the occasional ten-minute "brain break" into your busy schedule. Write out your schedule for tomorrow and include a plan to take some creative breaks. Experiment with listening to your favorite music, creative doodling, meditation, or stretching exercises to promote relaxation and incubation. In addition to hourly breaks, be sure to enjoy some kind of weekly "Sabbath" and to take a true vacation every year.

Trust Your Gut

Bring more attention to your everyday hunches and intuitions. Try writing them down in your Notebook and then checking your accuracy. Monitoring your daily intuitions will help you build confidence in your inner guidance system. You can strengthen your confidence further by listening to your body. Comments such as "My gut tells me otherwise," "I just know it in my bones," "I can feel it in the pit of my stomach," "I know in my heart of hearts that it must be true," reflect the body-centered nature of intuition.

When you take time for solitude—walking in nature, driving in your car, or just lying in bed—remember to listen to your bones and check in with your heart of hearts. Try the following exquisitely simple exercise, one or two times every day, for accessing the subtle nuances of your intuition:

Enjoy a few deep exhalations.

Soften your belly.

Be receptive.

Notebook Practice:
RECORD YOUR DREAMS

Keep your Notebook next to your bed when you go to sleep so you can write in it when your dreams are still fresh. People who record their dreams tend to be more in touch with their intuitive and creative powers. In a study at the University of British Columbia, students signed up for a course on creativity. At the beginning of the term, they were given an extensive battery of creativity tests, followed by just one assignment: to record their dreams and discuss them with fellow students during class time. At the end of term, the students took another battery of creativity tests and their scores improved by more than 25 percent.

Bohr, Coleridge, Dali, Descartes, Jung, Poe, and many others point to dreams as the wellspring of their genius. As Mozart commented, "All this inventing, this producing, takes place in a pleasing, lively dream." Elias Howe, the inventor of the modern sewing machine, got the idea for putting the eye at the end of the needle, instead of the middle, from cannibals who were boiling him for supper in one of his dreams. The cannibals had little holes at the ends of their spears.

Remembering your dreams is easier than you might imagine:

—Before you go to sleep, say to yourself: "Tonight I will remember my dreams."

—Upon awakening, allow yourself to "drift" for a few minutes with your eyes closed. With an attitude of gentle receptivity, scan your mind for pieces of your dreams.

—Note the elements of your dream in your Notebook. Do not expect them to make sense right away; just jot down the images, scenes, impressions, key words, or phrases that the dream suggests.

—Make a mind map. Many people find that making a mind map helps them recreate the dream material more efficiently and memorably.

—Interpret your dreams. The Talmud suggests that "a dream uninterpreted is like a letter unopened." If you want to interpret your dream, pretend that you are talking to the world's greatest psychiatrist and that she keeps asking you: "So tell me, what does this dream mean to you?" Write your response in your Notebook in stream-of-consciousness style.

Arte/Scienza

*The Development of the Balance between
Science and Art, Logic and Imagination.
"Whole-Brain" Thinking.*

"Study the science of art and the art of science."

—LEONARDO

The self-assessment questions in this section are designed to help you get a rough idea of your "hemispheric proclivities." Spend a few minutes reflecting on the statements in the self-assessment below. Which statements apply to you?

Self-Assesment: Arte/Scienza

- ❑ I like details.
- ❑ I am almost always on time.
- ❑ I am skilled at math.
- ❑ I rely on logic.
- ❑ I write clearly.
- ❑ Friends describe me as very articulate.
- ❑ Analysis is one of my strengths.
- ❑ I am organized and disciplined.
- ❑ I like lists.
- ❑ I read a book starting at page 1 and go through in order.

- ❑ I am highly imaginative.
- ❑ I am good at brainstorming.
- ❑ I often say or do the unexpected.
- ❑ I love to doodle.
- ❑ In school, I was better at geometry than algebra.
- ❑ I read a book by skipping around.
- ❑ I prefer to look at the big picture and leave the details to someone else.
- ❑ I often lose track of time.
- ❑ I rely on intuition.

Which list describes you best? The first list is a classic description of someone who is more "left-brained." The second list contains characteristics associated with a more "right-brained" person. Of course, most people are more complex than this simple model suggests. Nevertheless, the metaphor of left and right is a useful tool for thinking about balance.

Whatever your hemispheric tendencies happen to be, the key to filling your full potential is the continuing discovery of balance.

While championing the application of the left hemisphere through his attention to detail, logic, mathematics, and intense practical analysis (one of his mottoes was *ostinate rigore* or obstinate rigor), Leonardo also urged his students to awaken the power of the right hemisphere in what was, then, an unprecedented way: "I shall not refrain," he wrote, "from offering in these precepts a new and speculative idea, which although it may seem trivial and almost laughable, is none the less of great value in quickening the spirit of invention. It is this: that you should look at certain walls stained with damp or at stones of uneven color [elsewhere he suggests the study of the smoke and embers of a fire, of clouds and mud], . . . you will be able to see in these the likeness of divine landscapes . . . and an infinity of things [he mentions "figures in quick movement, and strange expressions of faces, and outlandish costumes] which you will be able to reduce to their complete and proper forms. With such walls and blends of different stones it comes about as it does with the sound of bells, in whose clanging you may discover every name and word that you can imagine."

This instruction represents more than just advice to stimulate an artist's imagination. It is a breakthrough in the evolution of human thought. Da Vinci gave birth to a tradition that resulted in the modern discipline of "brainstorming." Prior to Leonardo the concept of "creative thinking" as an intellectual discipline didn't exist.

Let's explore the notion of creative thinking by trying the following simple exercise:

Alternate Use Test 1

In two minutes, write down as many uses as you possibly can for a scarf. Do this now in the space below:

How many uses did you write down? Take the total number of answers and divide by two to calculate your score in terms of uses per minute. After you have calculated your score in uses per minute, circle your best answer. "Best" as you define it, using your own personal, subjective criteria.

The international average score (after dividing by two) is 4. A score of 8 is excellent and a score of 12 or more correlates significantly with other genius-level measures of idea generation.

What criteria did you use for choosing your best answer? Individuals with a strong left hemisphere dominance tend to struggle with this test. They write down three or four answers and choose their best answer based on logic and practicality. Individuals with a strong right-brain dominance tend to be more comfortable with this exercise and usually choose their favorite answer because it was the most imaginative or "far out."

Does the Alternate Use Test really test creativity? No. It tests one's comfort with free association; and, free association is a very important aspect of the creative process.

One of the most distinguishing characteristics of geniuses from all walks of life is the ability to shift back and forth from Arte—imaginative free association—to Scienza—logic and careful analysis. Geniuses intuitively understand the importance of letting the mind go outside of traditional constraints; they balance logic and imagination, freedom and discipline, left and right hemispheres.

Once you understand, as Leonardo did, the secret of free association, you know how to get your mind "out-of-the-box." Then, *after* you generate the "infinity" of ideas to which the maestro referred, you can use your analytical powers "to reduce them to their complete and proper forms."

Alternate Use Test 2

Try the Alternative Use Test again in the space below. This time, in two minutes, write down as many uses as you possibly can for an orange. To think like Leonardo, you'll focus on "an infinity of things." In other words, treat this as a test of *writing speed*. Write down answers as fast as you can without analysis or criticism. Then after you have generated a genius-level score, go back and use your imagination to explain your "off-the-wall" answers.

All of the exercises in this Workbook are designed to help you balance your hemispheres and awaken your latent Da Vincian capabilities. The exercise in this section focuses on one simple, tremendously powerful method for cultivating a synergy between Arte and Scienza in your everyday thinking, planning, and problem solving. The method is called **mind mapping**.

Mind mapping is a whole-brain method for generating and organizing ideas, originated by Tony Buzan, and largely inspired by Da Vinci's approach to note taking. You can use mind mapping for personal goal setting, interpersonal problem solving, writing business plans, even improving your children's performance in school. The most marvelous application of mind mapping, however, is that through regular practice it trains you to be a more balanced thinker, à la Leonardo.

Mind Mapping: "Straight from Nature"

Try the following exercise in understanding the nature of your mind: Think about the last book you read, or the last seminar you attended. Imagine that you have to write a report on that book or seminar. Begin recalling the information. As you do, observe the process of your mind at work. **Describe, briefly, the inner workings of your mind, as you try to recall your book or seminar, here:**

Does your mind work by constructing whole paragraphs or by presenting ordered outlines to your mind's eye? Probably not. Chances are that impressions, key words, and images float into your mind, one associating with the next. Mind mapping is a method for continuing this natural thinking process on paper.

Leonardo urged artists and scientists to "go straight to nature" in the search for knowledge and understanding. If you contemplate the structure of a tree, or a plant like the star-of-Bethlehem, you can see that it is a network of life, expanding in all directions from its trunk or stem. Take a helicopter ride over a major city; it is a sprawling structure of interconnecting centers and pathways, main arteries connecting with side roads. Our water table, global telecommunications system, and solar system are similarly linked networks. The structure of communication in nature is nonlinear and self-organizing; it works through networks and systems.

Perhaps the most amazing natural system of all is right inside your skull. The basic structural unit of brain function is the neuron. Each of our billions of neurons branches out from a center, called the nucleus. Each branch, or dendrite (from *dendron,* meaning "tree"), is covered with little nodes called "dendritic spines." As we think, electrochemical "information" jumps across the tiny gap between spines. This junction is called a synapse. Our thinking is a function of a vast network of synaptic patterns. A mind map is a graphic expression of these natural patterns of the brain.

It should not be too surprising, therefore, that the note-taking styles of many of history's great brains—such as Charles Darwin, Michelangelo, Mark Twain, and, of course, Leonardo da Vinci—feature a branching, organic structure complemented by lots of sketches, creative doodles, and key words.

At the end of the "Treatise on Painting," Leonardo wrote: "These rules are intended to help you to a free and good judgement: for good judgement proceeds from good understanding, and good understanding comes from reason trained by good rules, and good rules are the children of sound experience, which is the common mother of all the sciences and arts."

The rules of mind mapping are "intended to help you to a free and good judgement." They are "the children of sound experience," having been extensively tested and refined over the past thirty years.

Make a Mind Map

As you experiment with mind mapping, its advantages will become increasingly obvious. Mind mapping allows you to start quickly and generate more ideas in less time. Its free-ranging format—adding words to one branch one moment, then skipping over to another branch the next—increases your chances of generating new ideas. Mind mapping activates Arte and Scienza—your whole brain. It lets you develop a logical sequence and detailed organization of your material while encouraging imagination and spontaneity.

To help you get started, here is a simple mind-mapping exercise:

1. *Begin with the next page and six or more colored pens.*
   You may want to use phosphorescent highlighters for extra color.
2. *Place the Workbook horizontally in front of you.* A horizontal position makes it easier for you to keep all your key words upright and easy to read.
3. Let's say that the topic for this mind map is "The Seven Da Vincian Principles." Start your mind map by drawing a representative image in the middle of the paper. For this map, that has already been done for you

Mind Mapping: The Rules

1. **Begin your mind map with a *symbol* or a *picture* (representing your topic) at the *center* of your page.**
   Starting at the center opens your mind to a full 360 degrees of association. Pictures and symbols are much easier to remember than words. Drawing a picture or symbol stimulates your right hemisphere and strengthens your ability to think creatively about your subject.

2. **Use key words.**
   Key words are the information-rich "nuggets" of recall and creative association. Choosing key words exercises your analytical "left brain" and helps you find the essence of your subject.

3. **Connect the key words with lines radiating from your central image.**
   By linking words with lines ("branches"), you'll show clearly how one key word relates to another.

4. **Print your key words.**
   Printing is easier to read and remember than writing.

5. **Print *one* key word per line.**
   By doing this, you free yourself to discover the maximum number of creative associations for each key word. The discipline of one word per line also trains you to focus on the most appropriate key word, enhancing the precision of your thought and minimizing clutter.

6. **Print your key words *on* the lines and make the length of the word the same as the line it is on.**
   This maximizes clarity of association and encourages economy of space.

7. **Use colors, pictures, dimension, and codes for greater association and emphasis.** Highlight important points and illustrate relationships between different branches of your mind map. You might, for instance, prioritize your main points through color-coding, highlighting in yellow the most important points, using blue for secondary points, and so forth. Pictures and images, preferably in vivid color, should be used wherever possible; they stimulate your creative association and greatly enhance your memory.

4. Now *print key words or draw images on lines radiating out from your central image.* (Remember to print *on* the lines, *one* key word or image per line, and keep the lines *connected*.) To help you get started, you'll find the key word for some of the principles. Fill in the key words for the missing principles and make up an image to go with each one.

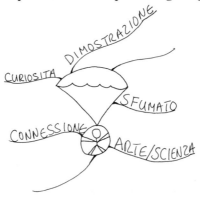

5. Working through free association, print key words on lines radiating out from your major branches; a few "secondary" branches are filled in for you to help you get the idea. Let your mind work freely by association and have fun.

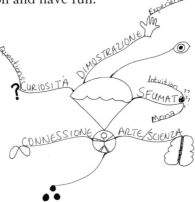

After you have filled your mind map with an abundance of key words and images, take a break. When you return to it, look for relationships that help you organize and integrate your ideas. Connect related parts of your mind map with arrows, codes, and colors.

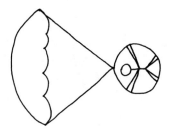

Practice Your Mind-Mapping Skills

Although mind mapping is an invaluable tool for simplifying complex tasks such as strategic planning, presentation preparation, meeting management, test preparation, and systems analysis, it is probably best to make your first few mind maps on relatively simple, lighthearted subjects. Choose one of the following topics to begin practicing your mind-mapping skill, solo, on the next page. Take about twenty minutes for this first practice map.

Mind Map Your Favorite Movie. Begin with a simple drawing that represents your favorite movie score. Print key words and draw images that express the characters, plot, and themes. Remember to put key words and images on lines radiating out from your central symbol.

Mind Map Your Dream House. Explore the delightful fantasy of a dream house using a mind map. Start with a symbol of your paradise in the center and then branch out with key words and images that represent the elements of your ideal living environment. Remember, let your mind work by association instead of trying to put things down in order. Just generate ideas for your ideal environment. Then after you have come up with a multitude of possibilities, you can go back and put them in order.

Mind Map Your Ideal Hobby. Use a mind map to make a plan for doing your ideal hobby. Start with an image in the center that represents your activity. Then use key words or images to represent the elements of your plan, such as materials, benefits, timing, etc.

Make a Mind-Mapping Mind Map. Okay, now that you have completed your first mind map, try making a mind map on all possible uses of mind mapping. Start with an image in the center of the page that represents the concept of mind mapping for you. Then branch out, putting printed key words or images on connected lines. Aim to generate at least twenty *specific* possible applications of mind mapping in your personal and professional life. After you have completed your mind map, highlight what you think might be the most valuable applications.

Keep the Following Tips in Mind. Keep your central image in the center of the page and limit its size. Use angled and curved lines as necessary in order to keep all your key words upright and easy to read. Use just *one* word per line and be sure to ***print*** the key words. Make the lines a bit thicker at their origin and print your letters at least one-quarter inch in height so they are easy to read. You can print some letters even larger for emphasis. Make each word the same size as the line underneath it. This saves space and allows you to see connections more clearly. If possible, use large sheets of paper. This helps to avoid crowding and encourages you to think big. Do not be concerned if your first draft seems disorganized. You can make a second or third draft for further clarification.

Know when to stop. Theoretically, a mind map never ends. As Da Vinci emphasized, "everything is connected to everything else." If you had the time, energy, inclination, enough colored pens, and a big enough piece of paper, you could go on linking all your knowledge and ultimately all human knowledge. Of course, if you are planning a speech or studying for an examination, you probably don't have time to link all human knowledge. The simple answer is that your mind map is finished when the information you have generated meets your objectives for the task at hand.

Make your "applications mind map" on the next page:

Corporalita

The Cultivation of Grace, Ambidexterity, Fitness, and Poise.

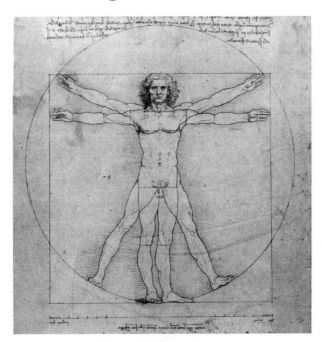

"Learn to preserve your health!."

— LEONARDO

If you go to your local library or bookstore to find a good book on holistic health, you'll discover that it contains many ideas that Leonardo recorded in his notebook 500 years ago. Da Vinci believed that we should accept personal responsibility for our health and well-being. He recognized the effect of attitudes and emotions on physiology (anticipating the discipline of psychoneuroimmunology) and counseled independence from doctors and medicines. He viewed sickness as "the discord of the elements infused into the living body." And viewed healing as "the restoration of discordant elements."

What is your personal approach to cultivating well-being and developing mind/body coordination? How can you optimize your fitness program? Begin by considering the following self-assessment.

Self-Assessment: Corporalita

❑ I am aerobically fit.
❑ I am getting stronger.
❑ My flexibility is improving.
❑ I know when my body is tense or relaxed.
❑ I am knowledgable about diet and nutrition.
❑ Friends would describe me as graceful.
❑ I am becoming more ambidextrous.
❑ I am aware of the ways in which my physical state affects my attitudes.
❑ I am aware of the ways in which my attitudes affect my physical state.
❑ I have a good understanding of practical anatomy.
❑ I am well coordinated.
❑ I love to move.

Da Vinci's life was an expression of the ancient classical ideal of *mens sana in corpore sano*: a sound mind in a sound body. Modern scientific studies confirm many of Da Vinci's recommendations, practices, and intuitions. Although it is a bit difficult to picture the maestro in a modern aerobics class, a personal fitness program is, nonetheless, a cornerstone of physical health, mental acuity, and emotional well-being. To actualize your potential as a Renaissance man or woman, maintain a balanced fitness program, like the one described in *How to Think like Leonardo da Vinci*. A healthy diet and aerobic, strength, and flexibility training are key elements in achieving and maintaining well-being; but your fitness regimen is incomplete without a constructive approach to body awareness, poise, and ambidexterity. These elements form the "missing link" in many fitness programs and are the focus of the exercises in this book.

Start with Unconditional Love and Self-Acceptance

A holistic approach to fitness begins with self-acceptance. We all know people who are always on a diet but never satisfied with their weight, people who pump iron relentlessly but never achieve enough definition. Health clubs are filled with people flogging themselves into exhaustion in search of an elusive state of perfection.

What is your image of your own body? How much are you influenced by external factors—magazine articles, the fashion industry, images on television, other people's opinions—in determining your own body image? Whatever your God-given strengths or weaknesses, you can dramatically improve the quality of your life by applying some Sfumato thinking to your fitness program: make a commitment to improve, grounded in unconditional self-acceptance.

Write your thoughts on the following statements in the space provided:

The message I receive(d) about my body from my mother

The message I receive(d) about my body from my father

The message I receive(d) about my body from my siblings

The message I receive(d) about my body from my lover

The message I received about my body from my peers

The message I receive(d) about my body from magazines, TV, and movies

Reflect on the messages you have received about your body and free yourself from anything you don't want, or your reactiveness against those messages. This may sound too simple but, as F. M. Alexander once wrote: "You can free yourself from the habits of a lifetime in a few minutes if you'll only use your brain."

In the spaces below write some the aspects of your physical being that inspire gratitude:

I am grateful for my _____

I am grateful for my _____

I am grateful for my _____

I am grateful for my _____

I am grateful for my _____

I am grateful for my _____

I am grateful for my _____

I am grateful for my _____

On the path of self-development, people commonly contemplate the classic question "Who am I?" You can make significant progress in self-realization by asking an even more basic question "Where am I?" Body image and body awareness play a tremendous role in determining self-image and self-awareness. In the Sensazione section, you were introduced to a program of exercises for sharpening the five senses: sight, hearing, smell, taste, and touch. Cultivation of body awareness begins with honing the sixth sense: kinesthesia. The kinesthetic sense is your sense of weight, position, and movement. It tells you whether you are relaxed or tense, awkward or graceful. You can begin to sharpen your kinesthetic sense and increase your self-awareness by experimenting with the following exercises:

Make a Drawing of Your Own Body. Make a sketch of your whole body in the space below. Don't wory about creating a masterpiece, just do a simple five-minute rendering; even a modified stick figure will be fine.

After you've sketched your whole body, color in red the places where you feel the most tension and stress. Then with a black marker, delineate the points in your body where your energy seems blocked, the parts where you feel the least. Next use a green color to indicate the areas of your body that feel most alive, where the energy flows most freely.

Most people have significant areas of red and black. Much of our unnecessary tension and stress is a result of ignorance and misinformation regarding our own natural structure and function. Inaccurate "body maps" result in misuse, exacerbating stress, and dulling awareness.

Mirror Observation. Stand in front of a full-length mirror (if you are courageous, do this naked). Avoid judging or evaluating your appearance, just observe your reflection objectively, and record your answers below:

Does your head tend to tilt to one side or the other?

Is one shoulder higher than the other?

Does your pelvis rock forward or is it held back?

Is your weight distributed evenly on your feet or do you depend on one leg more than the other for support?

What parts of your body appear to be overly tense?

Are your pelvis, torso, and head in a balanced alignment?

Heavy Thoughts

How much does your head weigh? Jot down your best guess.

Next time you are in the gym, pick up a fifteen-pound barbell, or when you visit the supermarket, hoist a fifteen-pound bag of potatoes. That is how much the average head weighs. This fifteen-pound globe contains your brain, eyes, ears, nose, mouth, and balance mechanism. What happens to your whole body if this globe is out of balance? What happens to your awareness and sensory acuity if your head is not properly aligned at the top of your spine? Did you know that 60 percent of your receptors for kinesthetic awareness is located in the neck? What happens to body awareness if the neck muscles are held in contraction to support a poorly balanced head?

Clearly, for the aspiring Renaissance man or woman, head balance is a top priority. You can deepen your appreciation for this question of balance with the following exercise.

Experience the Evolution of the Upright Posture

This exercise is inspired by the work of the great anatomist and anthropologist Professor Raymond Dart. It is particularly fun to do this exercise in a group but you can still get the value by doing it on your own. All you need is some clean, carpeted floor space and a towel.

Begin by lying facedown on the floor, with your feet together and your hands resting at your sides. (Put the towel under your face.) Notice that it is now impossible to fall. Rest facedown for a minute or two and contemplate the consciousness of a creature with this kind of relationship to gravity. Experiment with slithering along the floor toward an imaginary morsel of food.

Now get ready for an evolutionary leap. You are about to mutate. Slide the back of your hands along the floor beside you until they flip over so that your palms are now on the floor in front of you. Press down with your newly evolved paws to raise your head and upper torso off the ground. Look around and consider the leap in consciousness allowed by your expanded horizon. Experiment with using your paws to help you explore your environment and move toward food.

Next evolve to become a mammalian quadruped. Choose your favorite: horse, dog, cougar, gazelle, water buffalo. Move up onto all fours and, just for fun, imitate the gait, sounds, and other behaviors of your chosen animal. How does your range of behavior and potential awareness change in this position?

Your next huge evolutionary leap is to rise off your front paws and become a primate. Choose your favorite—chimpanzee, orangutan, gorilla—and enjoy moving around in monkey mode. How do the possibilities for awareness change? Does the changing relationship with gravity affect your options for communication and socialization?

Now rise up to your *full* stature as *Homo sapiens*.

Record your observations from this exercise here:

Write brief responses to the questions below in the spaces provided: What are the advantages and disadvantages of standing upright on two feet?

What are the implications of your upright posture for the development of intelligence and consciousness?

On a day-to-day basis, do you observe a relationship between people's posture and poise and their level of awareness and alertness?

Is it possible to feel depressed when you are fully upright? Can you feel joyous when you are slumped over?

Professor Dart, along with most of his colleagues, realized that our potential for consciousness and intelligence is intimately linked to the evolution of our fully upright stature. Yet the pressures of our lives—sitting in chairs, working at the computer, driving through rush hour—lead us to lose touch with this aspect of our birthright. For most of us, poise must be relearned.

Relearning Poise: Study the Alexander Technique

Leonardo was renowned for his effortless, upright poise and grace. The citizens of Florence turned out in numbers just to watch him walk down the street. Vasari enthuses about the maestro's "more than infinite grace in every action." It is almost impossible to imagine Leonardo da Vinci slumping and slouching around.

You can cultivate the Da Vincian qualities of poise, balance, and grace by studying the technique developed by another genius, F. Matthias Alexander. Born in Tasmania in 1869, Alexander was a Shakespearean actor specializing in one-man shows of tragedy and comedy. His promising career was interrupted by a tendency to lose his voice in the middle of performances.

When the doctors and coaches couldn't help him, Alexander realized that he must find a way to overcome his problem on his own, reasoning that something he was doing with and to himself was causing the problem. He began to observe himself in specially constructed mirrors. After many months of detailed and thorough observation, he noticed a pattern of tension and contraction that emerged the moment he *thought* of reciting. Alexander realized that he had to "unlearn" this pattern, reeducating his mind and body as a whole system in order to change. He discovered that the key to doing this was to ***pause prior to action,*** inhibiting his habitual pattern of contraction, and then focus on specific "directions" he evolved to facilitate a lengthening and expansion of his stature.

With repeated practice of this new method, Alexander not only regained full control of his voice, he also recovered from a number of persistent health problems and became famous on the stage for the quality of his voice, breathing, and stage presence.

People began to flock to Alexander for lessons, and he was able to assist these people in a surprising number of instances by helping them to eliminate the habits of ***inappropriate effort*** responsible for their maladies.

Alexander's work was also a profound influence on notables such as Aldous Huxley, George Bernard Shaw, John Dewey, and Nobel prize–winning scientists Sir Charles Sherrington and Nikolaas Tinbergen.

The Alexander work begins with a keen level of self-observation: Working in your Notebook, keep a diary of the appropriateness of your effort in everyday activities. Watch for ***inappropriate effort*** in activities such as sitting, bending, lifting, walking, driving, eating, and talking. Are you stiffening your neck and pulling your head back, raising your shoulders, narrowing your back, bracing your knees, or holding your breath in order to:

- pick up your toothbrush
- work at the computer
- talk on the telephone
- pick up a pen to write
- meet someone new
- speak in public
- hit a tennis, golf, or racquet ball
- tie your shoes
- turn your steering wheel
- bend down to pick something up
- take a bite of food

If you have ever seen a jogger lumbering painfully down the street, or witnessed the contortions of someone trying to lift weights that are too heavy, then you are familiar with what the philosopher John Dewey called "compensatory maladjustments." In other words, exercise without body awareness and poise can do more harm than good.

It is very difficult to observe and change these everyday habits without external feedback. Using a mirror or video can be quite helpful, but the best way to accelerate your progress is to take private lessons with a qualified teacher of the Alexander technique. Alexander teachers are trained to use their hands in an extraordinarily subtle and delicate way to guide you to free your neck, rediscover your natural alignment, and awaken your kinesthetic sensitivity.

In the meantime, you can use the following procedure, inspired by Alexander's work, to begin cultivating everyday poise and balance.

The Balanced Resting State

All you need to benefit from this procedure is a relatively quiet place, some carpeted floor space, a few paperback books, and ten to twenty minutes.

Begin by placing the books on the floor. Stand approximately your body's length away from the books with your feet shoulder-width apart. Let your hands rest gently at your sides. Facing away from the books, look straight ahead with a soft, alert focus. Pause for a few moments.

Think of allowing your neck to be free so that your head can go forward and up and your whole torso can lengthen and widen. Breathing freely, become aware of the contact of your feet on the floor and notice the distance from your feet to the top of your head. Keep your eyes open and alive, and listen to the sounds around you.

Maintaining this awareness, move lightly and quickly so that you are resting on one knee. Then sit on the floor so that you are supporting yourself with your hands behind you, feet flat on the floor and knees bent. Continue breathing easily.

Let your head drop forward a tiny bit to ensure that you are not tightening your neck muscles and pulling your head back.

Then gently roll your spine along the floor so that your head rests on the books. The books should be positioned so that they support your head at the place where your neck ends and your head begins. If your head is not well positioned, reach back with one hand and support your head while using the other hand to place the books in the proper position. Add or take books away until you find a height that encourages a gentle lengthening of your neck muscles. Your feet remain flat on the floor, with your knees pointing up to the ceiling and your hands resting on the floor or loosely folded on your chest. Allow the weight of your body to be fully supported by the floor.

To reap the benefit of this procedure, rest in this position for ten to twenty minutes. As you rest, gravity will be lengthening your spine and realigning your torso. Keep your eyes open to avoid dozing off. You may wish to bring your attention to the flow of your breathing and to the gentle pulsation of your whole body. Be aware of the ground supporting your back, allowing your shoulders to rest as your back widens. Let your neck be free as your whole body lengthens and expands.

After you have rested for ten to twenty minutes, get up slowly, being careful to avoid stiffening or shortening your body as you return to a standing position. In order to achieve a smooth transition, decide when you are going to move and then gently roll over onto your front, maintaining your new sense of integration and expansion. Ease your way into a crawling position, and then back onto one knee. With your head leading the movement upward, stand up.

Pause for a few moments . . . listen . . . eyes alive. Again, feel your feet on the floor, and notice the distance between your feet and the top of your head. You may be surprised to discover that the distance has expanded. As you move into the activities of your day, imagine moving with the grace of a figure painted by the maestro.

For best results, practice the Balanced Resting State twice a day. You can do it when you wake up in the morning, when you come home from work, or before retiring at night. The procedure is especially valuable when you feel overworked or stressed and before or after exercise. Regular practice will help you develop an upright, easy poise that encourages balance and grace in everything you do.

Notebook Practice:
DRAW MOVEMENT

As Leonardo probed the depths of nature, he saw that everything is changing and moving all the time. His drawings possess an inner dynamism that expresses this fundamental quality of movement, even in objects that appear to be still. In this exercise, observe the "essential movement" in an object as it falls. Drop tissues, a scarf, napkins, leaves, or a feather . . . and watch them fall. Ideally, sit by a waterfall for a few hours or just run a bath and watch the water come out of the faucet. Make "falling objects" a theme for the day. Aim to discover at least three new observations about falling bodies. Record your observations in your Notebook.

Then experiment with drawing the "tracks" of the movement of a falling object. Imagine feeling these tracks in your own body. Leonardo suggested the following: "Make some silhouettes out of cardboard in various forms and throw them from the top of the terrace through the air; then draw the movements each makes at the different stages of its descent." Marcel Duchamp's *Nude Descending a Staircase* was inspired by this Da Vincian exercise in seeing.

Find a nice spot to sit in a public place—train stations and airports are ideal—and watch people move. Practice the following exercise suggested by the maestro: ". . . Keep a sharp lookout for figures in movement . . . and note down the main lines quickly: that is to say putting an O for the head and straight or bent lines for the arms and the same for the legs and trunk."

Cultivate Ambidexterity

Leonardo, a natural left-hander, regularly switched hands when working on the *Last Supper* and other masterpieces.

Begin your investigation of ambidexterity by exploring the power of your nondominant hand. Try the following exercises.

Reverse Crossing. Practice interlocking your fingers and crossing your arms and legs in reverse of your normal pattern. See if you can wink your nondominant eye and roll your tongue over to *both* sides.

Use Your Nondominant Hand. Try using your nondominant hand for a day, or part of a day to start. Turn on the lights, brush your teeth, eat your breakfast, unlock your front door with your *other* hand. Record your feelings and observations in your Notebook.

Experiment with Writing. Try signing your name with the *other* hand here:

Now write out the alphabet with your nondominant hand:

Experiment with Writing and Drawing with Both Hands *Simulta-neously.* After you have a little practice writing with your nondominant hand, experiment with writing and drawing with both hands at once. Draw a few circles, triangles, and squares with both hands at once here:

Now try signing your name with both hands at the same time here:

Experiment with Mirror Writing. You will be surprised how easy it is to learn; all it takes is a little practice. Here is a sample to guide you. Copy the sample and then write a few lines on your own here:

[Handwritten mirror writing, best reading reversed:]

*My grandmother's wonderful name
was Bottonegie, and my mother's
wonderful name was Di-Lippe. My
name is Joan Pett and I more
... to write backwards ...
... to write. Maybe that's why my
son, Michael, has always been
interested in favorite Da Vinci,*

Cross-Lateral Refresher. To refresh your attention when learning, working, or struggling with a creative challenge: Reach behind your back and touch your right foot with your left hand and then your left foot with your right hand. Do this ten times. Or raise your left knee to touch your right hand, and then your right knee to touch your left hand. Do this ten times.

Ambidextrous Breathing. You can cultivate brain-body balance by practicing a technique based on ancient yogic wisdom and modern scientific understanding: alternate-nostril breathing.

Research shows that left-nostril breathing stimulates the right-brain and vice versa. By alternating from left to right, you inspire hemispheric coherence. Sit in an upright position, close your eyes, and then begin by blocking the flow of air into your right nostril by depressing it with your thumb or index finger as you exhale slowly through the left, then inhale through your left. Now close off your left nostril and exhale slowly through your right side. Keep the left blocked and inhale through the right. Then exhale through the left, inhale through the left, exhale through the right and so on. Try this alternate-nostril breathing for up to three minutes at a time, twice a day. (If you feel dizzy or uncomfortable in any way, stop.) Most people find that this practice is both calming and energizing.

Learn to Juggle

Learning to juggle is a marvelous way to develop ambidexterity, balance, and mind-body coordination. Da Vinci biographer Antonina Valentin confirms that the maestro was a juggler. The art was part of the pageants and parties that he designed for his patrons and went hand-in-hand with his love of conjuring. Moreover, the basic juggling pattern that you will learn, is a *fantasie de vinci,* a knot or infinity symbol.

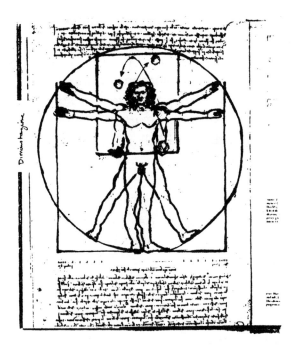

Get three balls (tennis balls are fine) and try the following:

1. Take one ball and toss it back and forth, from hand to hand, in a gentle arc just above your head.
2. Take two balls, one in each hand. Toss the ball in your right hand just as you did with one ball; when it reaches its high point, toss the ball in your left hand in exactly the same manner. Focus on smooth, easy throws and *let both balls drop*.
3. Same as step 2, only this time catch the first toss. Let the second one drop.
4. Same as step 2, only this time catch them both.
5. Now you are ready to try three balls. Take two balls in one hand and one in the other. Toss the front ball in the hand that has two. When it reaches it high point, throw the single ball in your other

hand. When it reaches its high point, throw the remaining ball. Let them all drop!

6. Same as step 5, only this time catch the first toss.
7. Same as step 5, only this time catch the first two tosses. If you catch the first two balls and remember to throw the third, *you will notice that there is only one ball remaining in the air,* and you can already do one ball. Catch the third ball and you will experience your first juggle. Celebrate!

Of course, once you achieve your first juggle, you will no doubt wish to experience multiple juggles. As you continue to practice, focus on the ease and direction of your throws and relax when the balls drop. If you keep your attention primarily on *throwing* and continue to breathe easily, your success will be inevitable.

Discover Your Center

Where do you locate your sense of your self? With the index finger of your left hand point to the place in your body that you identify with most strongly. Most Westerners point to their heads because of the Cartesian cognitive bias in our culture. Some people point to their hearts because they are more emotionally centered, but it is very rare for a Westerner to point to the belly as the locus of "self." In the East, it's usually the other way around. Eastern culture emphasizes that the belly is the center of one's being, the wellspring of the life force and intuitive intelligence. In Japan, the belly-center is called the "hara"; in China it's known as the "lower tan tien."

Leonardo's famous canon of proportion figure shows that the arms and legs are equidistant from the hara. The maestro's magnificent drawing celebrates the human center of gravity. You can improve your balance and poise by cultivating an awareness of your center. Begin by sitting or standing upright; press the point two-finger widths down from your navel. Then, inhale gently through your nose and send your breath down to your center, exhale slowly through your mouth maintaining an awareness of your center as you exhale. Do this seven times with full awareness to "center yourself"; and then remember to breathe into your center from time to time throughout the course of your day.

Practice Qi Gong

Leonardo viewed the elements of earth, fire, water, and air as the essences of creation. Qi Gong is an ancient Chinese discipline for drawing on the energy of the elements to strengthen your life force. It is the source of traditional approaches to healing and martial arts. It's best to learn Qi Gong directly from an authentic lineage master, but you can get an idea of this marvelous practice by practicing this simple energy warm-up exercise.

Stand upright, feet shoulder-width apart, shoulders relaxed, knees slightly bent. Enjoy a few cycles of breath into your lower tan tien. Keeping your feet firmly on the floor, hold your arms out at chest height, palms facing down; then exhale as you sink straight down by bending your knees, and inhale as you straighten up again. As you sink down and rise up rhythmically, imagine that you are drawing the energy of the earth through the soles of your feet. Feel the energy that grows a garden, sustains a forest or a field of golden wheat flowing up from the earth to fill every cell of your body. After eight repetitions, pause, then exhale as you reach your hands straight out from your chest, palms opening out as though you were reaching for the sun. Inhale as you draw your hands back toward your chest, imagining that you are filling your body with the healing golden light. Do eight repetitions and then pause.

Next bring your palms together in front of your chest, exhale as you open your arms out to the sides as wide as you can, inhale and bring your hands back to the center of your chest as you imagine washing all the molecules of your body with the wonderful energy of the ocean. Repeat for eight full cycles and then pause, and raise both arms straight up over your head. Bring your arms down in a big circle as you exhale, raise your arms straight up again and imagine filling your circle with the energy of the sky, stars, and new moon. Repeat eight times, pause, then raise your arms straight up as you inhale and bring them straight down as you exhale and imagine concentrating all the energy of the earth, sun, ocean, and sky—the whole universe—into your center.

In addition to the Alexander technique, juggling, and Qi Gong, other wonderful disciplines for cultivating Corporalita include the Japanese martial art of aikido, hatha yoga, tai chi, the Feldenkrais method, and the Pilates system of exercise.

Connessione

*A Recognition of and Appreciation for
the Interconnectedness of all Things
and Phenomena. Systems Thinking.*

"Everything is connected to everything else."

—LEONARDO

Students of spiritual practice know that the classical experience of enlightenment as described by Buddhist monks, Hindu gurus, Christian mystics, Aboriginal shamans, Sufi sheiks, and Hebrew Kabalists is characterized by two universal elements: radiant light and an experience of oneness with creation. As Leonardo probed the depths of truth and beauty he saw connections everywhere; he studied the way sound and aroma travel through air and the parallels in flowing water, and the curl of hair, the growth of plants, the formation of the bones and muscles and their realtionship to movement in humans and animals. He expressed his enlightenment in his masterpieces. Suffused with mystic, radiant light, they speak of a transcendental oneness, a unity of creation: Connessione.

This final series of exercises aims to give you practical tools for bringing the enlightenment of Connessione in your life, every day. Start by contemplating the self-assessment below.

Self-Assessment: Connessione

❑ I am ecologically aware.
❑ I enjoy similies, analogies, and metaphor.
❑ I frequently make connections that other people don't see.
❑ When I travel I am struck more by people's similarities than their differences.
❑ I seek a "holistic" approach to diet, health, and healing.
❑ I have a well-developed sense of proportion.
❑ I can articulate the systems dynamics—the patterns, connections, and networks—in my family and workplace.
❑ My life goals and priorities are formulated clearly and integrated with my values and sense of purpose.
❑ I sometimes experience a sense of connectedness with all creation.

Contemplating Wholeness. What does wholeness mean to you? Experiment with expressing your concept of wholeness in a drawing or doodle here:

List three situations in which you feel connected to something greater than yourself and your personal worries and concerns:

    1.

    2.

    3.

List three situations in which you feel disconnected from something greater than yourself:

    1.

    2.

    3.

Do you experience conflicts between the different parts of your self? In other words, do your mind, emotions, and body ever disagree? If so, which part tends to dominate? Describe some of the dynamics of your head, heart, and body, then try diagramming them in the space provided:

Escape from Incompleteness. Do a ten-minute stream-of-consciousness writing session (try this exercise with your nondominant hand; this will offer you a different way of thinking about things, a way that helps you access your intuition) on Leonardo's observation that "**every part is disposed to unite with the whole, that it may thereby escape from its own incompleteness.**" How does this apply to you?

Family Dynamics. Contemporary psychology emphasizes the importance of understanding the "systems dynamics" of your family in order to better understand yourself. In the space below, sketch a diagram that represents the dynamics of your family:

Jot down your reflections on the following questions about your family: What roles does each person play?

How are the roles interdependent?

What are the benefits of the family distribution of roles?

What are the costs?

What happens to the dynamics under stress?

What patterns have been handed down over generations?

What are the primary outside forces that affect the family dynamics?

What were the dynamics like one year ago . . . seven years ago? How have they changed? What will they be like in a year . . . in seven years?

How do the patterns of functioning you learned in your family affect the way you participate in other groups?

The Body Metaphor. Try using Leonardo's favorite metaphor—the human body—to further explore the dynamics of your family system by answering the questions below:

Who is the head?

Who is the heart?

Is the head in balance with the body?

What is the quality of our nourishment?

How well do we digest and assimilate nourishment?

How effectively do we process waste?

How is our circulation? Are our arteries sclerotic?

What is our backbone?

What are our sharpest senses? Our dullest?

Does the right hand know what the left hand is doing?

What is our state of health? Do we have chronic maladies, natural growing pains, or a life-threatening disease?

What are we doing, or what can we do, to become more fit, strong, flexible, and poised?

Making Dragons

The ability to see relationships and patterns, and make unfamiliar combinations and connections, is the core of creativity. Leonardo's wonderful dragons, and many of his innovations and designs, arose from the fanciful connections he made between seemingly unrelated things. You can develop your Da Vincian powers by looking at things that at first glance seem unrelated, and finding different ways to link them.

For example, what connections can you make between:

A bullfrog and the Internet? The frog's feet are webbed. The Internet links you to the World Wide Web

An Oriental rug and psychotherapy? Oriental rugs have complex repeating patterns and so does your psyche.

Get the idea? Aim to generate three or four connections for each of the following. This exercise is a great warm-up for individual and team brainstorming sessions. Have fun.

An ice cream cone and the human eye

A frown and an ocean liner

A cow and the Renaissance

Mathematics and humor

A Mozart concerto and a bottle of wine

A spider and a mind map

Sketches of flying birds and a whirlpool

Leonardo's flying machine and a computer

Samurai warriors and the game of chess

Ballet and rain

Autumn and curly hair

The environment and a honeybee

Imaginary Dialogues

Hillary Clinton was ridiculed by the press a few years ago for her imaginary dialogue with Eleanor Roosevelt. But "talking" with an imaginary role model is a time-honored and very effective to way to gain insight and perspective. It was recommended by the great Italian poet Petrarch and practiced enthusiastically in the Academy of Lorenzo de' Medici.

Choose a problem you wish to work on or an issue you want to understand in more depth. In addition to contemplating the maestro's views, you can also imagine the perspective that might be offered by any of your role models, "anti-role models," or perhaps by one of the great minds from history. You can have even more fun and further stimulate your creativity by imagining discussions on your problem or issue between different characters. Imagine a dialogue on your issue by, for example:

Warren Buffet and Hildegard von Bingen

Don Imus and Socrates

Amelia Earhart and Leonardo

Edgar Degas and Martha Graham

Colin Powell and Napoleon

Ted Hughes and Shakespeare

Martin Luther King and Gandhi

Any combination of characters you would like

Origin-all Thinking

Thinking about the origins of things is a marvelous way to appreciate Connessione. The modern Rennaissance genius Buckminster Fuller was known for enthralling audiences with his amazing improvisational presentations. Instead of preparing a lecture, Fuller would invite his audience to suggest a topic, anything at all. In one typical session, a college student suggested that Fuller speak about a Styrofoam cup. Fuller kept his audience spellbound for the next two hours as he discussed the origins of the cup: the chemical engineering advances that led to the invention of Styrofoam, the economic and social forces related to its manufacture, and their cultural and environmental implications.

Choose one of the following objects and consider all the elements involved in its creation:

+ This book
+ The clothes you are wearing now
+ Your watch
+ Your computer
+ Your wallet or purse

Express your thoughts in mind-map form on the next page. (If you do this exercise from time to time, and continue to probe and explore the deeper origins of things, you cannot help realizing that, as the maestro emphasized, "everything is connected to everything else.")

Notebook Practice:
THEME OBSERVATION

Winston Churchill once said, "Even pudding needs a theme!" Bring more meaning to your life by working with a theme. Awaken your Da Vincian powers by choosing a theme for the day, or week, and record observations in your Notebook. You can jot down your thoughts throughout the day, or make mental notes to be recorded in your Notebook at a quiet time before sleep. Aim to make accurate, nonevaluative observations. Speculation, opinion, and theory are fine, but actual observation offers the richest resource.

Your structured Workbook exercises will provide you with plenty of themes with which to work. For added benefit, choose a theme with a friend and compare notes at the end of the day. A powerful theme to begin with is "nonjudgmental awareness." Spend a day noting how you judge things as Good or Bad, Like or Dislike. Experiment with suspending that binary approach and just looking at things, especially other people, without judgment. What happens to your awareness and perception when you let go of these habitual categories?

Connessione Meditation

The sometimes frantic pace of our lives can, of course, lead us to lose touch with the microcosm and the macrocosm. It is hard to remember cosmic truths when you are rushing to meet a deadline, cleaning up after your kids, or fighting your way through rush-hour traffic. The following simple meditation offers another way to bring the experience of Connessione to your life every day.

Find a quiet place and sit down with your feet squarely on the floor, spine lengthening up. Close your eyes and bring your attention to the flow of your breathing. Be aware of the feeling of the air against your nostrils as you inhale. Exhale through your nose and feel the air flow out. (If your sinuses are stuffy, it's okay to breathe out through your mouth.) Keep your attention on the flow of your breathing, without trying to change it. Sit for ten to twenty minutes, just following your breath. If your mind wanders, bring it back to the immediate sensation of the breath.

Sitting quietly and meditating on the flow of breathing for twenty minutes will do you a world of good. But twenty minutes aren't always easy to find. So whenever you remember, in the course of your day, bring your awareness to your breathing. On busy days aim to pause once or twice and be fully present for seven breaths. When you are very busy, aim to be conscious for at least one full breath in the course of your day. These little oases of consciousness help connect you to yourself, to nature, to creation.

Time Line: River of Life

History books frequently offer time lines of significant events, chronicling an era or the life of a major figure. Making a personal time line is a marvelous tool for seeing the big picture of your life. On the next page make time lines for your life, including all the events you deem significant physically (birth, illness, childbearing, growth); mentally (key moments of understanding, insight, learning); emotionally (milestones of love, sadness, joy, depression); spiriually (experiences of communion, grace, transcendence, oneness); and globally (key events in your lifetime such as, perhaps, the fall of the Soviet Union).

Physical time line:

Mental time line:

Emotional time line:

Spiritual time line:

Global time line:

After you have sketched out the time line of your existence, experiment with imagining your life as a river. Visualize a source, perhaps the snow crystals on a mountain. Your destination, for this life, is the ocean.

Describe the dams, levees, eddies, whirlpools, rapids, and waterfalls of life so far. What are the major confluences with other rivers and bodies of water. How deep is your river? How pure? Does it ever freeze, almost dry up, or overflow its banks? How much flows underground? Is it teeming with life, providing sustenance for those who dwell on its shores? Look at the course of your life. Leonardo noted, "In rivers, the water you touch is the last of what has passed and the first of that which comes: so it is with time present."

Use your power of choice, in this present moment, to direct the course and quality of the river of your life.

Try a five-minute nondominant-handed stream-of-consciousness writing session on "my life as a river" here:

"Think Well to the End"

Leonardo was the ultimate "idea man." Although his practical skills in all areas are unsurpassed, his greatest strength was not to be found in implementation. Nevertheless, as he aged and became aware of his own mortality, he increasingly emphasized the importance of setting clear goals and following through to completion. In his later years he wrote repeatedly: "Think well to the end" and "Consider first the end." He even drew a representation of his personal goals.

You can set and achieve your goals more effectively with the help of a simple acronym: make all your goals SMART.

S *Specific:* Define exactly what you want to accomplish, in detail.

M *Measurable:* Decide how you will measure your progress, and, most importantly, how you will know that you have achieved your goal.

A *Accountablilty:* Make a full commitment to be personally responsible for achieving your goal. When setting goals in a team, be certain that accountability is clear.

R *Realistic and Relevant:* Set goals that are ambitious but achievable; as Leonardo noted, "We ought not to desire the impossible." Check that your goals are *relevant* to your overall sense of purpose and values.

T *Time Line:* Create a clear time line for the achievement of your goals.

Before you embark on the final exercise, which will include guidance for setting SMART goals for your life, let's set the stage by "thinking well to the end." Consider the legacy you would like to leave. Imagine hovering in space looking down at your own funeral. List the people that you would ideally like to be present: family, friends, mentors, students, bosses, employees, professional associates, and members of your community:

Next to each person's name write a sentence that expresses how you would like them to remember you:

In interviews with older people, most express much more regret for things they *did not do* rather than the other way around. Make a list of things you might especially regret not doing in this lifetime:

Write an inscription for your urn or tombstone:

If you had just six months left to live, what would you be sure to do:

Make a Master Mind Map of Your Life

One of the aims of this book is to provide you with tools to live your life as a work of art. To help you realize this aim, complete the following exercise for making a work of art about your life.

In this final exercise you will look at your life—your goals, values, priorities, and purpose—from a Connessione perspective. It is all too easy to go through life without *comprehensively* considering what we want. Of course, we all think about our careers, relationships, and finances from time to time. And many people devote significant time to crafting visions, goals, and strategies at work. But rarely, if ever, do we contemplate all our personal goals and *how they fit together.*

To get the most from this potentially life-changing exercise I recommend that you devote a minimum of an hour a day over the course of seven days. The seven days do not have to be consecutive, but you should aim to complete the whole exercise within three weeks. Set up your equivalent of the maestro's studio: instead of brush and canvas, you will use colored felt-tip pens, this Workbook, and a few large sheets of blank white paper. Work to the sounds of inspiring music and fill the air with your favorite aromas.

If you have already done this before, don't worry—your life mind map will look different every time. Compare the two when you're finished and do a five-minute stream-of-consciousness exercises on their differences in your Notebook.

DAY ONE: SKETCHING THE BIG PICTURE OF YOUR DREAMS

Create Your Own "Impresa" (*impresa*: emblem). An impresa was the personal "logo" of scholars, nobles, and princes during the Renaissance. Make up your own personal impresa or logo. Take your time and allow a resonant image to emerge from within. Doodle or sketch your ideas for an impresa on the following pages. This impresa will become the central **image of your life mind map.**

Make a "Sprezzatura" Map of Your Goals (*sprezzatura*: nonchalance; related to casual drawing or "sketching").

Draw your impresa in the center of the next page. On lines radiating out from this central image, print a key word or sketch a symbol for each of your life's major areas, such as people, career, finances, home, possessions, spirituality, fun, health, service, travel, learning, and self. (Express these life areas in any terms you like; feel free to add, delete, or change the categories suggested here.) Make this first version a sprezzatura or nonchalant sketch of the "big picture" of your life. Ask yourself, "What do I want?" in each of these areas.

Look at your first casual draft and ask: "Have I expressed all the areas that are important to me? If I could have, do, or be anything at all, what would it be?"

DAY TWO: EXPLORING YOUR GOALS

Begin by drawing your impresa in the center of the next page. Now, do a more organized mind map of your life goals, with vivid, multicolored images for each of your major life areas. Radiating from each of your main branches (i.e., Finances, Health, etc.), print key words or draw other images that begin to express your goals for each branch in more detail.

Begin exploring *each branch by writing brief answers to the following questions in the spaces provided:*

People. What relationships are most important to me? What qualities would my relationships have ideally?

Career. What is my ultimate career goal? What are my interim goals? What would my ideal job or career be?

Finances. How much money do I need to support all my other goals and priorities?

Home. What is my ideal living environment?

Possessions. What stuff is important to me?

Spirituality. What kind of relationship would I like to have with the Divine? How can I become more susceptible to Grace?

Health. What shape would I like to be in? What is the quality of energy I want?

Fun. What would give me the greatest delight?

Service. What contributions do I dream of making to others?

Travel. Where do I want to go?

Learning. If I could learn anything at all, what would it be?

Self. What kind of person would I like to be? What qualities would I like to cultivate?

Use all your senses to create a vivid image of what you want in each area.

DAY THREE:
CLARIFYING YOUR CORE VALUES

Your goals represent your response to the question "What do I want?" Your understanding of your values arises from considering "Why do I want it?" Look at each of your goals, contemplating the questions "Why do I want this? Why is it important? What will the realization of this goal bring to my life?"

Ask yourself: "How much of what I want is determined by my conditioning, the messages I have internalized from parents, priests, and pundits? How much of what I want is determined by my reaction or rebellion against my conditioning? How much of what I really want springs from my essence, independent of conditioning or reaction to it?"

As you contemplate the deeper motivations underlying your goals, your core values begin to come into focus. This exercise is designed to accentuate that focus. The following list contains some key words that represent values. (Please add your own key words to the list at any time.) Read through the whole list and notice your response to each key word.

achievement	excitement	insight	passion	spontaneity
adventure	expression	integrity	patriotism	stability
authenticity	family	justice	perfection	status
awareness	fashion	kindness	playfulness	subtlety
beauty	freedom	knowledge	pleasure	teaching
charity	friendship	leadership	power	time
community	fun	learning	recognition	tradition
compassion	generosity	loyalty	religion	truth
competition	growth	love	respect	winning
creativity	honesty	money	responsibility	wisdom
discipline	humility	nature	security	working
diversity	humor	novelty	sensitivity	
ecology	imagination	order	serenity	
excellence	independence	originality	spirituality	

Which words resonate most strongly with you? Highlight ten, then list them, in order of importance to you, below:

1.   6.
2.   7.
3.   8.
4.   9.
5.   10.

Reflect on your list of ten values before writing brief answers to the following questions. What areas of your life provide the truest expression of your values?

What areas lead you away from what you value?

How are your values mirrored in your goals?

Next, create an image or symbol that represents each of your core values.

DAY FOUR:
CONTEMPLATING YOUR PURPOSE

Some people seem to be born with a clear sense of purpose. Leonardo, for example, always organized his life around the quest for truth and beauty. Most of us, however, require a lot of contemplation to understand the meaning and purpose of our lives. The secret of discovering your life's purpose is to hold the question *"What is my purpose?"* in your mind and heart until enlightenment strikes. While you are waiting, try the following to make yourself more susceptible to enlightenment:

In the space that follows do a stream-of-consciousness writing session on "What my purpose is *not!*" This will help you define the "negative space" around what *is* your purpose.

Experiment with writing a "Statement of Purpose" in twenty-five words or less. Just give it your best shot. Then rewrite it once a month until you feel a frisson of focused energy through your whole body when you read it.

You know you are on the right track when all your cells say: "Yes!"

Write your Statement of Purpose here:

DAY FIVE:
LOOKING FOR CONNECTIONS

On a large sheet of blank paper, make a new mind map that includes all your goals, and branches for Values and Purpose. **Draw your impresa and other images with care. Make them as vivid and beautiful as possible.** After expressing your life goals, values, and purpose in mind-map form, write out your thoughts on the following questions in the spaces provided:

Do I have clear, specific goals?

Can I measure my progress toward acheiving my goals?

Are my goals realistic and relevant to my purpose and values?

Are my goals *in proportion*—do they all fit together and support one another? The maestro wrote: "Proportion is not only to be found in number and measure, but also in sounds, weights, times and places, and in every power that exists."

What are my top priorities (list your goals in order of importance)?

DAY SIX:
ASSESSING CURRENT REALITY

Does your current mode of working, relating, learning, loving, relaxing, and budgeting time and money contribute to the achievement of goals? Review the major areas of your life, assessing your current status as objectively as possible. (For added perspective, solicit feedback from someone you trust.) Write three lines in response to the following questions:

People. What are my relationships like now? How can I have the quality of communication in my most important relationships?

Career. What is the current state of my career?

Finances. What is my financial status? What are my assets, debts, income, and earning potential?

Home. What is my living situation now?

Possessions. What stuff do I have?

Spirituality. What relationship do I have with God?

Health. What kind of shape am I in? What is the quality of my energy now?

Fun. Am I enjoying life?

Service. What contributions do I make to others?

Travel. Where have I been?

Learning. What are the biggest gaps in my education?

Self. What kind of person am I now? What are my strengths and weaknesses?

Values. What is the difference between the values I would like to have and those that, judging from my actions and behavior, I actually have now?

As you complete your assessment of your life as it is now, answer the following questions in three lines or less:

Where are the greatest gaps between what I want and what I've got?

Am I "on course" for realizing my most important goals? What "course adjustments" do I need to make to bring my life into balance?

Now, the most important question for artists of life:

Am I willing to embrace Sfumato, to hold the creative tension between my highest ideals and goals and my current reality?

If you are in debt, it's hard to imagine abundance. If you are recovering from a painful breakup, it isn't easy to picture yourself in a fulfilling relationship. And if you're suffering from a serious illness, it's a challenge to visualize perfect health; but it is when we are faced with adversity that our willingness to embrace a positive forward path is most significant.

Twenty-five years ago, six friends and I were traveling through Southern Italy on a slow train. It was hot and crowded, but we didn't mind because we were young and drinking wine from a gallon jug. At a tiny station outside Naples, the train grunted and then stopped. A gray-haired couple walked slowly toward us. The old man helped his partner onto the stairs and then stepped back to say good-bye. Bent over, she made it halfway up the stairs when she looked up and saw a trainful of hairy, wine-sodden youths. Her face dropped and she turned back to the old man with eyes pleading for relief from her fate. The old man paused, looked her deeply in the eyes, and whispered one word: "*Corràgio.*" The old lady straightened up, set her jaw, and walked onto the train. Courage—*corràgio*—is a quality of the heart. It is the willingness to "get on board" despite adversity; to embrace a positive vision in the face of pain and fear.

Of course, it is much easier to hold the tension between ideals and reality, to find *corràgio,* if you have a strategy for closing the gap.

DAY SEVEN:
STRATEGIZING FOR CHANGE

You define your goals and vision by contemplating the question "What do I want?"

You clarify your values and purpose by contemplating the question "Why do I want it?"

You craft a strategy by answering the question *"How* will I get it?"

Working backward from your ideal eulogy, go through your goals and consider the resources and investments you will need for realizing each one.

Now in the space below, translate your life mind map into a one-year plan:

When you have completed your one-year mind map, review your goals and make sure they are SMART.

Then create an affirmation for each of your major life areas. Write your affirmations below:

Now decide the steps you will take this week, *today,* toward realizing each of your goals. Write out the changes you will make in the space provided:

At the beginning of each week, invest twenty to thirty minutes and make a mind map of your weekly goals, priorities, and plans. If you like, you can color-code each of your major life areas. This gives you instant visual feedback on your success in balancing your priorities. Make your first weekly mind map here:

Look at the whole picture of your weekly plan. Is your week a balanced rainbow or a monochromatic blur? Have you planned enough time for nurturing your relationships, your health, your personal and spiritual development?

As you survey your weekly map, ask how each activity you have planned supports the realization of your purpose and values.

Finally, each day, make a mind map of your daily plan. If you can devote just ten to fifteen minutes at the start of your day, or the evening before, to mind mapping your goals and priorities, you'll be better able to take a Connessione approach to your everyday challenges.

Intrinsic Values

We live in a world that values results and acheivements more than beauty and being. It is easy to lose oneself in the quest for success. The Da Vincian principles are useful tools for accomplishing your goals and improving your performance in life, but their deeper meaning is to be found in savoring the experience of living. Leonardo's quest was for the essence of truth and beauty. Why did he leave so much unfinished? Partly because he was more interested in the process of questing than in its product. Many of his ideas and an unknown number of his works have been lost forever, but, to paraphrase Ionesco, "Sometimes the ephemeral is the only thing of lasting value." More than his acheivements, Leonardo's greatest gift to humanity is his supreme inspiration for reach to exceed grasp . . . he beckons us to look at our lives and remember that, "to enjoy [is] to love a thing for its own sake and for no other reason."

On September 10, 1499 Leonardo's twenty-rour-foot-high clay model of the Sforza Equestrian monument was destroyed by invading French troops. Five hundred years later, the horse is reincarnated, thanks to the vision of Charles Dent. Before his death in 1994, Dent, a pilot, art collector, and Renaissance man, founded an organization of scholars, sculptors, and idealists dedicated to recreating Da Vinci's lost masterpiece. *Il Cavallo* lives as a symbol of the pure expression of the Da Vincian love of life, truth, and beauty. If you would like to be part of this remarkable project contact LDVHI, Inc., P.O. Box 396, Fogelsville, PA. 18051-0396. Telephone: 610-395-4060.

RESOURCES

Wine Tasting
To learn more about wine tasting, get Michael Broadbent's *Complete Guide to Wine Tasting and Wine Cellars*, published by Simon & Schuster, New York, 1984, or Marian W. Baldy's *The University Wine Course,* published by the Wine Appreciation Guild, San Francisco, 1993.

To find the best wines to taste, subscribe to Robert Parker's "The Wine Advocate," P.O. Box 311, Monkton, MD 21111. Telephone: (410) 329-6477. Fax: (410) 357-4504.

Learning to Draw
Renowned educator Dr. Betty Edwards and her associates offer seminars in drawing and perceptual skills throughout the U.S. Contact:
DRSB
1158 26th Street, Suite 530
Santa Monica, CA 90403
or
contact Visionary Artist and Master Teacher Lorraine Gill c/o The Brain Foundation

The Alexander Technique
To find a certified teacher of the Alexander technique, contact: the American Society of Teachers of the Alexander Technique—NASTAT—401 E. Market Street, Charlottesville, VA 22902 (804) 295-2840.

Visual Synthesis
Simultaneous, artistic illustration of the content of meetings, conferences, and strategic planning sessions. Contact:
Nusa Maal c/o I.M.I.
Telephone: (301) 652-8464

To attend a public program or arrange a presentation/workshop for your organization on how to think like Leonardo da Vinci, contact:

Michael J. Gelb, President
The High Performance Learning® Center
114 The Promenade
Edgewater, NJ 07020
Telephone: (201) 943-5303
E-mail: DaVincian@aol.com
Web page: http://www.michaelgelb.com

ABOUT THE HIGH PERFORMANCE LEARNING® (HPL) CENTER

An international leadership training and consulting firm founded by Michael J. Gelb in 1982, HPL guides individuals and organizations to define and realize their highest aspirations. HPL helps leaders build teamwork, creativity, communication, and organizational alignment. A catalyst for creative change, HPL bridges the gap between visions of exceptional quality, superior service, and personal fulfillment and everyday behavior. HPL's most popular programs and services (all customized to achieve specific client goals) include:

+ How to Think Like Leonardo da Vinci
+ Mind Mapping and Creative Problem Solving
+ High-Performance Presentations
+ Lessons from the Art of Juggling
+ Aikido in Daily Life; A Fresh Approach to Negotiation and Interpersonal Problem Solving
+ Samurai Chess: Secrets of Strategy (with Grand Master Raymond Keene O.B.E.)
+ The Executive Renaissance seminar

CONTACT

Michael J. Gelb
The High Performance Learning® Center
114 The Promenade
Edgewater, NJ 07020
Telephone: (201) 943-5303
E-mail: DaVincian@aol.com
Web page: http://www.michaelgelb.com

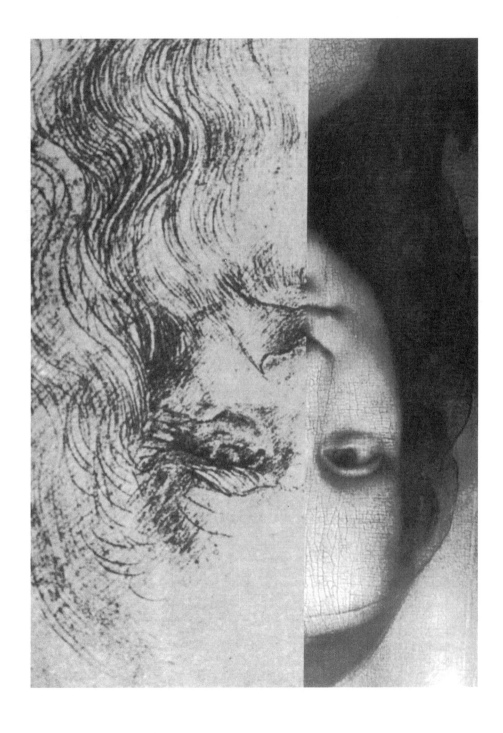

ABOUT THE AUTHOR

Michael Gelb is a globally acclaimed pioneer in the fields of accelerated learning, creative thinking, and leadership development. He is the president of High Performance Learning, an international management training and consulting firm based in the New York metropolitan area. Established in 1978, HPL's clients include AMEC, BP, Du Pont, KPMG, Merck, Microsoft, Nike, and Western Union. Michael Gelb is the author of the *New York Times* business bestseller *How to Think like Leonardo da Vinci*. Gelb is also the author of *The New Mind Map, Present Yourself: Captivate Your Audience with Great Presentations, Thinking for a Change,* and *Discover Your Genius: How to Think Like History's Ten Most Revolutionary Minds.* A third-degree black belt in the martial art of aikido, Gelb is co-author with chess grand master Raymond Keene of *Samurai Chess: Mastering Strategy Through the Martial Art of the Mind.* Michael Gelb's first book, *Body Learning: An Introduction to the Alexander Technique,* debuted in 1981 and has become the standard text in the field. A former professional juggler who once performed live with Mick Jagger and the Rolling Stones, Gelb is also the author of *More Balls Than Hands: Juggling Your Way to Success by Learning to Love Your Mistakes.*

Michael Gelb's work has been featured in *The New York Times, The London Review of Books, Executive Excellence, The Washington Post, USA Today, Investor's Business Daily, Industry Week,* and many other publications. He has appeared on *Good*

Morning America and many other television and radio programs, including *Talk of the Nation*, *The Diane Rehm Show,* and *The Connection*. Gelb was the co-recipient, with former senator John Glenn, of the 1999 Brain Foundation "Brain-of-the-Year" Award (previous winners include Stephen Hawking, Bill Gates, Garry Kasparov, and Gene Roddenberry). In 2002, Gelb received a Batten Fellowship, awarded by the University of Virginia's Darden Graduate School of Business. He has also lectured for George Mason University's executive MBA program and at the University of Pennsylvania's Wharton School.

"At the heart of each of us, whatever our imperfections, there exists a silent pulse of perfect rhythm, a complex of wave forms and resonances, which is absolutely individual and unique, and yet which connects us to everything in the universe."

"*Every part is disposed to unite with the whole, that it may thereby escape from its own incompleteness.*"

LEONARDO ON CONNESSIONE

"The earth and myself are of one mind."

NATIVE AMERICAN CHIEF ON CONNESSIONE

"Nothing less than becoming one with the universe will suffice."

MORIHEI UESHIBA ON CONNESSIONE

"Be really whole and all things will come to you."

LAO-TZU ON CONNESSIONE

"For he who would proceed aright . . . should begin in youth to visit beautiful forms . . . out of that he should create fair thoughts; and soon he will of himself perceive that the beauty of one form is akin to the beauty of another, and that beauty in every form is one and the same."

"All men are interdependent . . . . Our destinies are tied together."

MARTIN LUTHER KING ON CONNESSIONE

"The most perfect actions echo the patterns found in nature."

MORIHEI UESHIBA ON CONNESSIONE

"The so-called 'mental' and 'physical' are not separate entities . . . all training . . . . must be based on the indivisible unity of the human organism."

F. M. ALEXANDER ON CORPORALITA AND CONNESSIONE

"Keep your mind cheerful and avoid grievous moods."

"He who knows that power is inborn . . . and so perceiving throws himself unhesitatingly on his thought, instantly rights himself, stands in the erect position, commands his limbs, works miracles."

RALPH WALDO EMERSON ON CORPORALITA

"There are two kinds of people, those who put everyone into two groups and those who don't."

ECONOMIST KENNETH BOULDING ON ARTE/SCIENZA

"Depending on the circumstance, you should be hard as a diamond, flexible as a willow, smooth flowing like water, or as empty as space."

AIKIDO FOUNDER MORIHEI UESHIBA ON ARTE/SCIENZA

"It is by logic you prove, but by intuition that you discover."

MATHEMATICIAN HENRI POINCARÉ ON ARTE/SCIENZA

"Genius is the art of non-habitual thought."

WILLIAM JAMES ON ARTE/SCIENZA

"Order is the shape upon which beauty depends."

AUTHOR PEARL BUCK ON ARTE/SCIENZA

"The great and golden rule of art, as well as of life is this: That the more distinct, sharp and wiry the bounding line, the more perfect the work of art. . . . Singular and Particular Detail is the Foundation of the Sublime."

WILLIAM BLAKE ON ARTE/SCIENZA

"The test of a first-rate intelligence is the ability to hold two opposing ideas in mind at the same time and still retain the ability to function."

F. SCOTT FITZGERALD ON SFUMATO

"I bought a humidifier and a dehumidifier, put them in the same room, turned them on and let them fight it out."

"There are two kinds of truth: small truth and great truth. You can recognize a small truth because its opposite is a falsehood. The opposite of a great truth is another great truth."

NOBEL PRIZE—WINNING PHYSICIST NIELS BOHR ON SFUMATO

"To know one thing you must know the opposite."

SCULPTOR HENRY MOORE ON SFUMATO

"Doubt is uncomfortable, certainty is ridiculous."

"Confusion is the welcome mat at the door of creativity."

"Order comes out of disorder, form out of chaos,
as it did in the creation of the universe."

AUTHOR AND PSYCHOLOGIST ROLLO MAY ON SFUMATO

"One does not discover new lands without consenting to lose sight of the shore for a very long time."

AUTHOR ANDRÉ GIDE ON SFUMATO

"Sell your cleverness and buy bewilderment."

SUFI MASTER AND POET JALAL AL-DIN RUMI ON SFUMATO

"It is very beautiful here, if one only has an open and simple eye without any beams in it. But, if one has that it is beautiful everywhere."

VINCENT VAN GOGH ON *SAPER VEDERE*

"The lover is drawn by the thing loved, as
the sense is by that which it perceives. . . ."

LEONARDO ON SENSAZIONE

"Climb the mountains and get their good tidings; nature's peace will flow into you as sunshine into flowers; the winds will blow their freshness into you and the storms their energy; and cares will drop off like autumn leaves."

"Impressions washed quickly over him, fleeting and vivid; the vermillion glaze of a potter, the firmament crowded with stars which were also gods, the moon, from which a lion had fallen, the smoothness of marble under gentle feeling fingertips, the savor of boar's meat, which he loved to tear at with fierce white teeth, a word of the Phoenician language, the black shadow thrown by a lance on the yellow sand, closeness of the sea or of women, the heavy wine whose harshness balanced the taste of honey, could, one and all, define the whole range of his spirit. . . ."

JORGE LUIS BORGES ON SENSAZIONE

"The real magic lies not in seeing new landscapes, but in having new eyes."

AUTHOR MARCEL PROUST ON SENSAZIONE

"The five senses are the ministers of the soul."

"He who tastes, knows."

"A man's errors are his portals of discovery."

"By and large I seem to have made more mistakes than any others of whom I know, but have learned thereby to make ever swifter acknowledgement of the errors and thereafter immediately set about to deal more effectively with the truths disclosed by the acknowledgement of erroneous assumptions."

MODERN RENAISSANCE GENIUS BUCKMINSTER FULLER ON DIMOSTRAZIONE

"...rink without wine; sated without food; distraught; foodless and sleepless; a king beneath a humble cloak; a treasure within a ruin; not of air and earth; a sea without bounds. He has a hundred moons and skies. He is wise through universal truth, not a scholar from a book."

"Everyone wants to be right, but no one stops to consider if their idea of right is right."

F. M. ALEXANDER ON DIMOSTRAZIONE

On his deathbed he painted a picture of a flower. As he died, he mused, "I think I'm beginning to understand something about art."

"Every blade of grass has its angel that bends over it
and whispers, 'Grow, grow.'"

THE TALMUD ON CURIOSITÀ

"Life must be lived as play."

"In the master's secret mirror, even at the moment of highest renown and accomplishment, there is an image of the newest student in the class, eager for knowledge, willing to play the fool."

AUTHOR AND AIKIDOIST GEORGE LEONARD ON CURIOSITÀ

"I want to know how God created the world. I am not interested in this or that phenomenon, in the spectrum of this or that element. I want to know His thoughts, the rest are details."

EINSTEIN ON CURIOSITÀ

"Live the questions."

POET RAINER MARIA RILKE ON CURIOSITÀ

"You can tell whether a man is clever by his answers.

You can tell whether a man is wise by his questions."

NOBEL PRIZE—WINNER NAGUIB MAHFOUZ ON CURIOSITÀ

SAY YES!

Leonardo wrote about the value of writing in a notebook: "Feathers shall raise men even as they do birds, toward heaven; that is by letters written with their quills." In this, your *How to Think like Leonardo da Vinci Notebook,* you too will soar toward heaven. Similarly, the Sufi master Rumi—one of the many geniuses whose words will inspire you on the coming pages—wrote about the genius within: "Inside you there's an artist you don't know about. . . . Say yes quickly, if you know, if you've known it from the beginning of the universe."

Say yes to yourself, yes to life, yes to the genius within you and your children. Write your Yes! here! Sign and date this Yes! below:

....

Congratulations! You have made the first entry in your Da Vinci Notebook. Now, turn the page and keep going.

The How to Think like Leonardo da Vinci Notebook ⟶ᡠ